Systems Archetype Basics

Systems Archetype Basics

From Story to Structure

Daniel H. Kim
AND Virginia Anderson

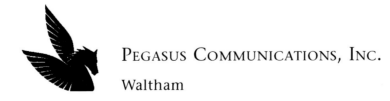

PEGASUS COMMUNICATIONS, INC.

Waltham

PEGASUS COMMUNICATIONS, INC.
One Moody Street
Waltham, MA 02453-5339 USA
Phone 800-272-0945 / 781-398-9700
Fax 781-894-7175
customerservice@pegasuscom.com   info@pegasuscom.com

www.pegasuscom.com

ISBN 10   1-883823-04-8
ISBN 13   978-1-883823-04-7

Acquiring editor: Kellie Wardman O'Reilly
Project editor: Lauren Johnson
Production, art, and design: Boynton Hue Studio

♻ Printed on recycled paper

Printed in Canada

Revised edition

11   10   10 9 8 7 6 5 4 3 2

5864

To the Reader: Why Use This Book?   vii

Section 1   **About the Systems Archetypes**   1

Section 2   **Fixes That Fail**   7

Section 3   **Shifting the Burden**   25

Section 4   **Limits to Success**   43

Section 5   **Drifting Goals**   61

Section 6   **Growth and Underinvestment**   73

Section 7   **Success to the Successful**   87

Section 8   **Escalation**   99

Section 9   **Tragedy of the Commons**   111

Section 10   **Using Archetypal Structures**   127

Section 11   **Additional Learning Activities**   139

Appendix A   **Potential Responses to the Learning Activities**   151

Appendix B   **A Palette of Systems Thinking Tools**   177

Appendix C   **Systems Archetypes at a Glance**   179

Appendix D   **Additional Resources**   183

Appendix E   **A Glossary of Systems Thinking Terms**   185

Why Use This Book?

Congratulations! By picking up this book, you've taken a major step in learning to use the systems archetypes. This powerful collection of systems thinking tools offers a highly effective way to grasp the complexities of organizational life and to address the stubborn, recurring problems that often confront us in the business world. *Systems Archetype Basics: From Story to Structure* is designed to help you discover the principles of the archetypes and begin actually using them. This workbook also builds on the first volume in The Pegasus Workbook Series: *Systems Thinking Basics: From Concepts to Causal Loops*, which focuses on the foundational principles of systems thinking and introduces behavior over time graphs and causal loop diagrams.

Why Systems Archetypes?

Why take time out of your busy schedule to read this workbook and complete the Learning Activities? Because the systems archetypes open a window onto important, recurring "stories" that happen in all walks of organizational life. The archetypes let us step back and see that many organizations—from small startups to huge, established companies—experience similar systemic challenges. Systems archetypes help us deepen our understanding of these challenges and design effective action plans for addressing them.

How to Use This Book

There are many ways to present the systems archetypes. In this book, we start with the more familiar, accessible ones and work our way up to the more complex ones. For this reason, we recommend that you read the sections in numerical order, although you're certainly free to choose a different order depending on your interests and familiarity with the material. We also hope that you'll collaborate as often as possible with others on the readings and the Learning Activities—working together often yields far more insights than puzzling through the concepts and exercises on your own.

Systems Archetype Basics begins with an introduction to the archetypes in general, including their history. The next eight sections explore the archetypes one by one. Each of these sections follows a similar structure: They begin with a story that captures the "signature" dynamic of that particular archetype. They then explain the archetype's storyline in general terms and explore the typical behavior over time of that archetype. Next, the sections introduce the archetype's systemic structure, or template, and show how to map the opening stories onto the template. Each section closes with tips for diagramming the archetype, a deeper look at what we can learn from the archetype, and guidelines for managing the dynamics of the archetype.

Section 10 goes more deeply into the many rich ways you can use and apply the archetypes, including tips on detecting particular archetypes at work. Section 11 contains additional Learning Activities for those readers interested in more practice. Finally, the workbook closes with a set of appendices that offer potential responses to all the Learning Activities, a summary of the 10 tools of systems thinking, a list of the archetypes "at a glance," an additional resources list, and a glossary of systems thinking terms.

About the Learning Activities

Mastering the systems archetypes requires lots of practice with real-life examples. Accordingly, almost all the sections in this workbook contain a wealth of illustrations from the business world and a series of Learning Activities that challenge you to apply your new knowledge. The Learning Activities can be done as self-study or in groups, though, again, we encourage you to work in groups as much as possible.

These Learning Activities generally start with a story. Then, you'll be asked to briefly summarize the archetypal theme in the story, identify key variables, graph the behavior of some of those variables over time, and create a causal loop diagram that depicts the archetypal, systemic structure manifested by the story. Each set of Learning Activities also ends with a special activity that invites you to choose a story from your own life that you feel demonstrates the particular archetype in question. As you complete these activities, remember that there are many ways to diagram a system. Try to focus more on understanding the nature of the archetypes rather than diagramming them "correctly." The Learning Activities, and the potential responses to them, are meant to spark your imagination and serve as a starting point for you to think about the archetypes.

Acknowledgments

The work contained in this book is built on the prior work of many others. First, we acknowledge Peter Senge for introducing the concept of system archetypes to a broad management audience in *The Fifth Discipline.* In many ways, the tremendous success of his book is what made the writing of this workbook possible in the first place. We also acknowledge all those who were involved in the development of these principles and concepts before they ever appeared in *The Fifth Discipline,* including John Sterman, John Morecroft, Michael Goodman, Jenny Kemeny, and David Kreutzer. In addition, we thank Peter Stroh, Sherry Immediato, Kristin Cobble, Donella Meadows, and all the workshop participants and *The Systems Thinker* contributors who have given us valuable insights into understanding and applying the archetypes. Finally, we honor Jay Forrester's brilliance and insight in founding the field of system dynamics, which we believe has much to contribute to the practice of management.

In addition, we're deeply grateful to the following people for reviewing early drafts of the sections and offering helpful suggestions for strengthening the presentation: Chaddus Bruce; Teresa Hogan, The Coca-Cola Company; Richard Karash, Karash Associates, Inc.; Renee Moorefield, The Coca-Cola Company; David Packer, the Systems Thinking Collaborative; Kristina Wile, the Systems Thinking Collaborative.

At Pegasus, we thank Kellie Wardman O'Reilly for helping us to envision and initiate this project, and Lauren Johnson, whose tireless and persistent efforts as project manager and editor were instrumental in producing this book with high quality and in a timely manner. Thanks also to Cia Boynton, for creating the attractive design and transforming the manuscript into a book, and to Scott Young for coordinating the printing cycle.

We hope you'll find your adventure into using the systems archetypes stimulating and rewarding on both a personal and professional level. We also invite you to contact us with any comments, questions, or suggestions about using this book or about the archetypes in general.

Enjoy!

Daniel H. Kim
(dhkim@alum.mit.edu)

Virginia ("Prinny") Anderson
(VRAnderson@aol.com)

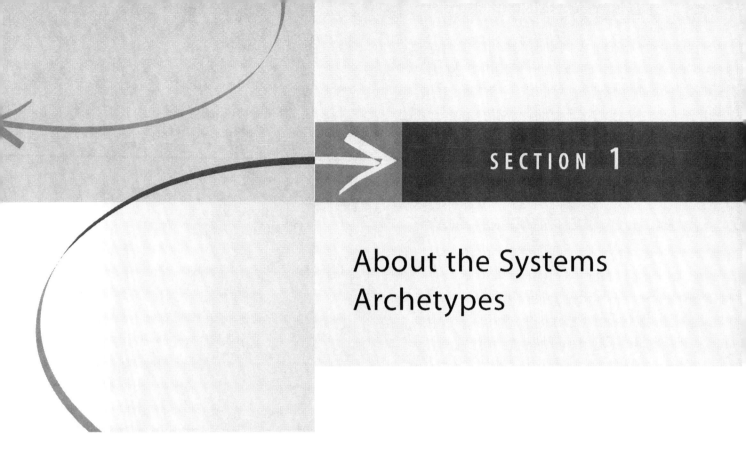

About the Systems Archetypes

WHAT IS A SYSTEMS ARCHETYPE?

Without having to climb beanstalks or push anyone into an oven, children learn lessons from fairy tales about how to hide from powerful, cruel beings, build solid dwellings, and be respectful of old people. Literary themes also show us the hero's journey, the trials of hard work, the outcomes of faithful love and misguided passion, and the ennui of a materialistic life. In these examples from literature, the term *archetype* signifies a recurring, generic character, symbol, or storyline. In systems thinking, the term has a very similar meaning. It refers to recurring, generic systemic structures that are found in many kinds of organizations, under many circumstances, and at different levels or scales, from internal personal dynamics to global international relations.

Captured in the stories, structures, and behavior over time of the archetypes are similar teachings about competition, addiction, the perils of quick fixes, and the high flyer's downfall. And as we do with stories and fairy tales, we can use the archetypes to explore generic problems and hone our awareness of the organizational dramas unfolding around us. We can even use archetypes to sharpen our ability to anticipate difficulties, communicate about them with our colleagues, and find ways to address them together.

The systems archetypes, as a group, make up one of the 10 current categories of systems thinking tools. (See Appendix B for a complete list of these tools.) Each archetype features a storyline with a distinctive theme, a particular pattern of behavior over time that can be graphed, and a unique systemic structure that can be depicted in a causal loop diagram. The value of archetypes is that we can study them apart from a specific story, problem, or organizational situation and take away generic, transferable learnings that we can then apply to many situations in our own lives.

WHERE DID ARCHETYPES COME FROM?

In the 1960s and 1970s, Jay Forrester, Dennis Meadows, Donella Meadows, and other pioneers of systems thinking observed several recurring systemic structures. In the 1980s, Michael Goodman, Charles Kiefer, Jenny Kemeny, and Peter Senge built on that work, in part with the help of notes developed by John Sterman, by describing, diagramming, and cataloguing these generic systemic structures as systems templates. When Peter Senge authored *The Fifth Discipline: The Art and Practice of the Learn-*

A REVIEW OF CAUSAL LOOP DIAGRAMS

Causal loop diagrams (CLDs) are graphic representations of our understanding of systemic structures. They're valuable because they reveal our thinking about how the system is constructed and how it behaves. When we share our CLDs with others, these diagrams become especially useful because they help us understand one another's thinking about how the system in question works.

Anatomy of a CLD

CLDs consist of one or more feedback loops that are either reinforcing or balancing processes. Each loop contains variable names that represent components of the system that change over time, cause-and-effect relationships among the variables, and delays (see Figure 1.1, "A Simple Causal Loop Diagram").

FIGURE 1.1

A Simple Causal Loop Diagram

[Figure: A circular causal loop diagram. Labels read: "cause-and-effect notation", "s", "variable", "Level of Job Stress", "B", "Use of Coping Strategies", "o", "balancing process notation", "link", "Delay".]

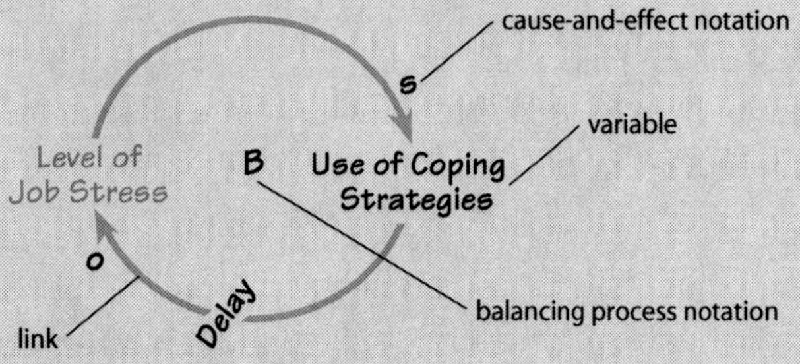

In Figure 1.1, the system is depicted as one feedback loop. The two variables that make up this system are "Level of Job Stress" and "Use of Coping Strategies." The "s" and "o" designate how each variable affects the other. The "s" means change in the *same* direction; "o" means change in the *opposite* direction. To "read" this diagram, we would say, "As level of job stress goes up, so does use of coping strategies. As use of coping strategies goes up, level of job stress goes *down*, after some delay." Note that we could also start off by thinking of job stress as going down: "As job stress decreases, so does use of coping strategies. As use of coping strategies decreases, job stress might then rise again eventually."

Balancing and Reinforcing Processes

Reinforcing and balancing processes are the building blocks of all the systems that we are part of and that we see around us. The "B" in the center of Figure 1.1 signifies that this particular feedback loop represents a balancing process. A *balancing* process tries to bring the system's behavior to a desired state and keep it there—much as a thermostat regulates the temperature in your house. These loops act as stabilizers within an overall system. In Figure 1.1, the level of job stress might therefore rise and fall somewhat over time, but in the long run it would stay roughly the same, around some implicit or *ing Organization*, he referred to those structures as systems archetypes. Since then, the notion of systems archetypes has become quite popularized, and systems thinking practitioners have continued to teach, apply, and write about these recurring generic structures as well as investigate and test the potential of identifying new ones.

HOW CAN YOU USE THE ARCHETYPES?

When you are trying to examine an issue, a problem, or a situation systemically, the numerous tools of systems thinking can help you in your inquiry. The systems archetypes, as one class of systems thinking tools, can open a whole new dimension of your learning. Because each archetype comes with its own storyline (or causal theory), pattern of behavior over time, and systemic structure depicted in a causal loop diagram (like templates), you can connect to it and apply its learnings from any of

explicit goal (see Figure 1.2, "A Balancing Process Over Time"). Balancing processes can also lead to dramatic oscillations, as extreme deviations in one direction create strong counterforces that then push that variable back toward the desired state. In complex systems, this adjustment process is rarely smooth. Instead, the countering actions often overshoot the goal, and the system oscillates back and forth, much like a pendulum.

A *reinforcing* process, by contrast, compounds change in one direction with even more change in that direction—creating exponential growth or collapse (see Figure 1.3, "A Reinforcing Process").

To "read" Figure 1.3, we could say, "As work anxiety increases, the rise in anxiety causes the number of mistakes made to increase, which makes anxiety even worse." Note that this reinforcing process can also work in a much more favorable direction: "As work anxiety *decreases*, so do number of mistakes made, which further eases anxiety" (a "virtuous" cycle as opposed to a "vicious" one!). Like balancing processes, reinforcing processes also have their own distinctive pattern of behavior over time (see Figure 1.4, "A Reinforcing Process Over Time"). This behavior is characterized by increases or decreases that occur at an ever-increasing rate.

FIGURE 1.2

A Balancing Process Over Time

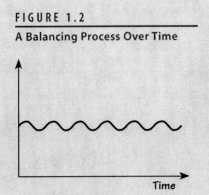

FIGURE 1.3

A Reinforcing Process

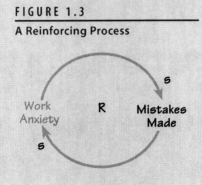

FIGURE 1.4

A Reinforcing Process Over Time

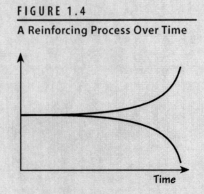

those entry points (see "A Review of Causal Loop Diagrams"). As you work on a problem—going over the story, identifying key variables, sketching causal loop diagrams—you may suddenly find that something about the story resonates with one or more of the archetypes, giving you a new key for unlocking part or all of your problem. At other moments, you may finish graphing the behavior over time of key variables, and notice a pattern that seems to match a behavior pattern associated with one of the archetypes. A rich vein of questions, theories, and possibilities opens up for your investigation. Or, you may be looking over a causal loop diagram drawn by a colleague and notice a particular combination of loops that reminds you of the core structure of a certain archetype, and that prompts you to ask a question that had not yet occurred to either of you.

At first, you'll probably find your own way of applying your understanding of the system archetypes—through using story themes, structure-behavior pairs, or generic causal loop diagrams. Eventually, you can use all three aspects of the archetypes to broaden your perspective on systemic problems, generate additional or unexpected questions, notice when you are experiencing one or more of these recurring dynamics, and anticipate possible future outcomes of current actions and events.

 ## WHO'S ON FIRST? WHAT'S ON SECOND?

In this workbook, we will cover eight systems archetypes. All eight consist of unique, distinctive combinations of reinforcing and balancing processes, and some of them build on each other. The eight archetypes are:

- Fixes That Fail
- Shifting the Burden
- Limits to Success
- Drifting Goals
- Growth and Underinvestment
- Success to the Successful
- Escalation
- Tragedy of the Commons

Many printed compilations of the systems archetypes list them in alphabetical order, which makes it easy to locate a particular one. However, when you're just beginning to learn about them, there's a way to present them that can help you see interrelationships among them, and make contrasts and comparisons. The first three archetypes presented in this book are generally the most easily recognizable—once you know them, you'll see them everywhere around you. They appear first in this book so that you'll be inclined to explore them first.

"Fixes That Fail" is the first archetype that we'll explore because it involves an activity that we all engage in frequently: problem-solving. It is followed by its close cousin, "Shifting the Burden," which takes you more deeply into inquiry about our tendency to apply quick fixes that focus on symptoms rather than on root causes. The third archetype we'll examine is "Limits to Success," which is especially relevant because of many organizations' tendency to be obsessed with growth for growth's sake, often without regard to any limits we might face. This archetype can help you manage the pressure to grow more realistically by helping you choose, anticipate, and prepare for inevitable limits.

The remaining archetypes appear in a particular sequence as well. Some of them are related to one or more of the first three in that they represent further elaboration or development. "Growth and Underinvestment," for example, is a combination of "Limits to Success" and one other archetype, "Drifting Goals." Other archetypes, like "Tragedy of the Commons" and "Escalation," tend to apply at the group or organizational level rather than at the intra- or interpersonal level.

With this quick overview in mind, let's move on to our first archetype: "Fixes That Fail"!

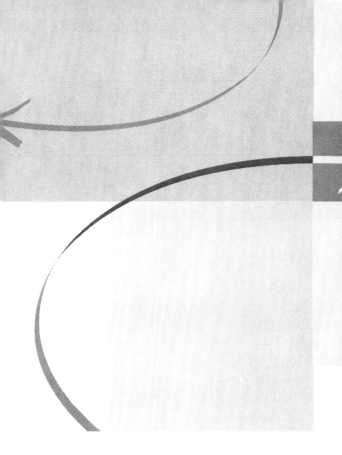

SECTION 2

Fixes That Fail

In a "Fixes That Fail" situation, a problem symptom cries out for resolution. A solution is quickly implemented, which alleviates the symptom. However, the solution produces unintended consequences that, after a delay, cause the original problem symptom to return to its previous level or even get worse. This development leads us to apply the same (or similar) fix again. This reinforcing cycle of fixes is the essence of "Fixes That Fail."

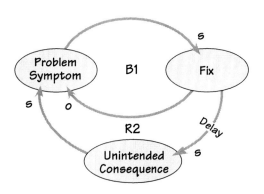

THE STORYLINE:

Borrow Now, Pay Later

It's a sad but not uncommon story. An energetic and determined entrepreneur with a good idea, a great service, or a new product sets up shop in his basement. He builds a prototype, scrapes together some cash, and marches out to sell his invention. Over the next few months, he takes a little more money from his savings account to get the business off the ground. With this cash to keep him going, he makes more contacts, maybe finds a customer or two. Unexpected costs for satisfying these customers arise, like modifications to his invention, installation, training, and so forth. To make ends meet before the revenue stream starts, he borrows on his credit card. Marketing is time consuming, not really his forte, so he hires someone to help out. He invests in a stock of raw materials so that he can

7

respond rapidly to the orders that are sure to pour in. His credit card payments grow higher and higher as the finance charges pile up, so he applies for a home equity loan to keep the business going.

You know how this story is likely to end. The undercapitalized small business venture addresses short-term cash needs with an ever-mounting debt, which solves the cash shortage for the moment but makes it worse over time—and perhaps even leads to bankruptcy.

"FIXES THAT FAIL" AT ALL LEVELS: AN ARCHETYPE FOR A NATION

Let's take the same story about the entrepreneur and project it to the scale of the national economy. Picture a nation whose spending programs at the federal and state levels exceed its revenues. The politicians decide to cover the shortfall by borrowing money to finance roads, defense, medical assistance, welfare, and a host of other programs and services. The following year, these expenditures include continuation of old projects, new promises to constituents, and payments on the earlier debt. Faced with the painful, possibly unpopular choice of cutting programs or of raising taxes (potentially an even more unpopular decision), the politicians take the easy way out and borrow again. As with the entrepreneur's predicament, you can guess how this story ends: The nation gets saddled with a multitrillion dollar debt, with the interest payments on that debt becoming a larger and larger portion of the federal budget.

OILING THE SQUEAKY WHEEL: THE GENERIC STORY BEHIND "FIXES THAT FAIL"[1]

The archetypal systemic structure called "Fixes That Fail" has been compared to oiling a squeaky wheel. When we detect a problem, we pick a fix that appears to work. However, we only pay attention to the short-term results of the fix—not the long-term (and more important) impact. We fall into reactive, "firefighting" mode, continually fixing squeaky wheels instead of making fundamental improvements.

Worse, in our haste to "fix the squeaking" (grabbing the "oil"), we may mistakenly pick up a can of "water" and splash it on the squeaky wheel. In the short term, even water will act as a lubricant and stop the squeaking. As the water evaporates and the metal rusts, however, the wheel begins to squeak again, but more loudly than before. We reach for the water—after all, it worked the last time. When there are finally no more squeaks, we may discover that instead of having fixed the problem, we have encased the wheel in rust.

Of course, we all know that oil or grease, not water, should be used to lubricate a squeaky wheel. But suppose the squeaky wheel is a powerful constituent, a dissatisfied customer, or a vigilant investment analyst. How do we know whether we are applying the oil or the water when we respond? Do we understand enough about the situation's "chemical reaction" to take appropriate actions? Or in our frenzy of fighting fires and oiling squeaky wheels, are we throwing *oil* on fires and applying *water* to wheels?

THE PROBLEM SYMPTOM: BEHAVIOR OVER TIME

Let's look carefully at the typical behavior over time of a "Fixes That Fail" situation. Remember: "Fixes That Fail" starts with a problem symptom, such as increasing revenue pressure, shrinking profits, growing customer complaints, or rising need for cash. If we were to graph the problem symptom's behavior over time, our graph would show a steadily rising or dropping curve (see Figure 2.1, "Behavior Over Time of a Problem Symptom").

At some point, the problem gets bad enough to be called a crisis, and we apply a fix. The problem symptom shows up in the behavior over time graph as a rising or falling curve punctuated by one or more dips or blips as the quick fix is applied (see Figure 2.2, "Application of the Quick Fix"). This pattern shows that a quick fix does indeed move things toward the desired state—for example, higher profits or lower number of customer complaints. However, if the unintended consequence of the fix makes the original problem worse, then the solution is only temporary. In such cases, the pattern of problematic behavior will soon return.

FIGURE 2.1

Behavior Over Time of a Problem Symptom

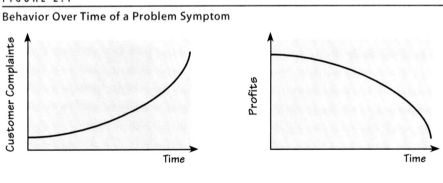

FIGURE 2.2

Application of the Quick Fix

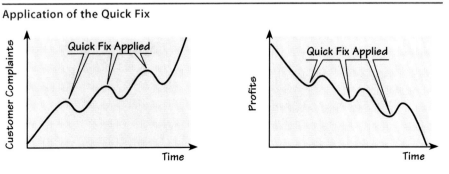

THE SYSTEMIC STRUCTURE BEHIND "FIXES THAT FAIL"

Like most archetypal structures, "Fixes That Fail" exhibits a two-part dynamic. First, the problem cries out for solution—something is not working the way it's supposed to, or is out of control. This first dynamic can be depicted as a balancing loop containing the problem symptom and quick fix (see loop B1 in Figure 2.3, "The Structure Behind 'Fixes That Fail'"). This balancing loop represents the theory about how we tend to solve problems.

The second part of the dynamic usually begins out of sight, and often unfolds relatively slowly. This part of the story is depicted in loop R2 in the diagram, and is the reinforcing process that comes as the unintended consequence of the fix.

Delay is another important component in the "Fixes That Fail" story—important because it has such a destructive impact. It often takes time for an unintended consequence to take effect. Furthermore, there may be an even longer delay before anyone notices the effect of the unintended consequence. People may even reapply the quick fix several times before anyone wonders why the problem symptom keeps recurring. By then, the whole systemic structure is well entrenched and hard to stop or turn around. Sometimes, the negative effects of the unintended consequence are irreversible.

So, to again "walk through" the archetypal structure behind "Fixes That Fail," we would start with the problem symptom. When the symptom arises, we apply a fix, which reduces the symptom (B1). The fix, however, leads (after a while) to an unintended consequence that actually *revives* or even *worsens* the problem symptom (R2).

FIGURE 2.3

The Structure Behind "Fixes That Fail"

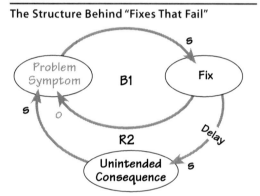

APPLYING STRUCTURE TO STORY

In "Fixes That Fail" situations, the problem we perceive and respond to is often the symptom of a deeper, less visible problem. For example, perhaps the entrepreneur's business plan was based on overly optimistic projections, or maybe he had no experience with some aspects of running a business. For the nation with a growing debt, the deeper problem may be that local interests are winning out over national interest, or that politicians are focusing more on getting reelected than on practicing good statecraft. In these cases, it makes sense to take a long, hard look at the deeper problem rather than merely treating the symptom.

Often, we are not aware of what's really causing the "wheel" to "squeak." Yet because Western business and social culture quickly rewards prompt, decisive action, we move rapidly to implement a solution that alleviates the symptom. The entrepreneur borrows from sources that make funds available quickly—savings, credit cards, and home equity. The politician advocates popular spending programs while denouncing higher taxes. Most of us tend to move quickly to quiet the squeaking wheel.

The relief is temporary, however, because the symptom comes back, often worse than before. The need for cash returns with the additional burden of repaying the debt, so the entrepreneur or national budget gets saddled with the weight of ever-increasing interest payments, and the wheel resumes squeaking.

What would the causal loop diagrams look like for the entrepreneur's story and the tale of the debt-ridden nation? In the case of the entrepreneur (see Figure 2.4, "The Entrepreneur"), the need for cash leads to borrowing, which temporarily eases the need for cash (B3). However, after a delay, the borrowing leads to higher interest costs and higher monthly payments, which only worsen the need for cash—the original problem (R4).

In the case of the debt-burdened nation (see Figure 2.5, "The Nation"), when the nation's thirst for federally funded programs gets higher than its current revenues, a budget deficit arises. Politicians find it easier to respond to this situation by engaging in deficit spending, which alleviates the budget pressure for the current year (B5). Of course, the current year's deficit increases the total debt and the consequent interest payments, which only worsen the budget pressure the following year (R6).

In both of these stories, the phenomenon of the worsening symptom stems from the unintended (or longer term) consequences of the solution. These consequences usually emerge over a long period of time and are reinforced by repeated application of the fix.

FIGURE 2.4

The Entrepreneur

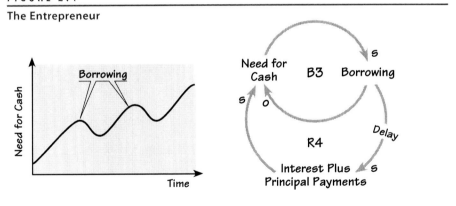

FIGURE 2.5

The Nation

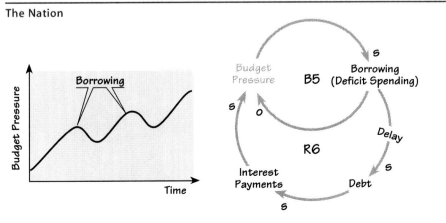

DIAGRAMMING "FIXES THAT FAIL"

How would you go about diagramming the systemic structure behind a "Fixes That Fail" situation? The first step is to identify and clarify what problem symptom you are trying to address and to examine the thinking about the various possibilities for fixing the problem. For example, the entrepreneur believed that borrowing money would solve the problem of inadequate cash flow. Remember that this initial thinking, or theory, is not completely wrong—the fix *does* work in the short run. However, it is usually based on an incomplete or short-sighted view of the situation. To diagram this part of the structure, you can represent your theory about solving the problem by linking the problem symptom with the fix in a balancing loop. You may find that, over time, several actions were taken to solve the problem. In that case, an easy way to represent this is to depict each fix separately in its own balancing loop by drawing a set of nested loops (see Figure 2.6, "Nested Loops").

FIGURE 2.6

Nested Loops

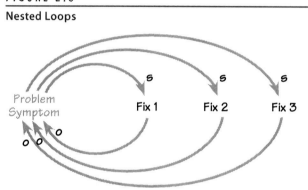

The second step is to identify the unintended consequence of the fix and determine how it develops. A key question you can ask is, "When I implement the solution and it reduces or eliminates the problem symptom, what are the longer term consequences that eventually affects the problem symptom?" Again, there may be several answers, all of which can be depicted by a set of nested loops. The key point here is to focus only on those consequences you believe will feed back in some way to cause the problem symptom to reappear or worsen.

 ## A DEEPER LOOK AT "FIXES THAT FAIL"

In a "Fixes That Fail" situation, the people closest to the problem often feel the pain of the situation most acutely and are motivated to reduce the pain as quickly as possible. They may even have a sense that the problem is part of a larger, deeper issue that has been getting worse over time. But, their main preoccupation is to reduce the pain as soon as possible and to worry about those deeper concerns later.

In many situations, it feels natural to just attend to each crisis as it happens, so as to bring the rising pressure under control. Whether people are aware of it or not, their sense of being caught in a reinforcing process has motivated them to create a balancing process, in which the intended function of the quick fix is to bring the problematic behavior back to an acceptable level.

As is often the case when people are under pressure, there may be little time to consider the deeper nature of the problem or think through whether the intended solution will produce the desired change. Indeed, the balancing structure does seem to work—for a while. If it did not, people wouldn't keep repeating the fix. However, quick fixes often require increasing amounts of effort, energy, and attention to keep the problem symptom under control.

The fix temporarily alleviates the problem symptom, but at what expense? Usually, it's a guarantee of more problems in the future. In some instances of "Fixes That Fail," people are aware of potential negative consequences of applying the quick fix. But the pain or cost of not doing something right away is more real and immediate than the impact of any delayed, undesirable outcomes. In other cases, people are unaware of the unintended consequences—an even more dangerous predicament.

Why is it so hard for people to see or attend to the unintended consequences of a quick fix? There are many reasons. Time delays between when the fix is applied and when those consequences show up can be quite long, making it difficult to connect cause and effect. We human beings are wired to pay attention to immediate threats to our survival, and we're less attuned to threats that unfold over a longer period of time. People may also avoid acknowledging unintended consequences in order to satisfy a political need for appearing decisive and achieving rapid, visible improvements. The cases of a politician close to reelection or a drive to reduce costs to meet shareholders' quarterly profit expectations are apt examples. Another reason is that people's mental models of how the system works and how the fix will play out are often incomplete or inaccurate.

Finally, the phenomenon of shifting loop dominance, which occurs in every systems archetype, starts to kick in: The energy or drive in the system shifts from the quick-fix loop to the unintended-consequences loop. The delayed and accumulated consequence of applying the quick fix takes over. Because this latter part of the dynamic is a reinforcing process, it can rapidly spiral into a vicious cycle, sometimes called "the death spiral." The painful irony of the "Fixes That Fail" dynamic is that the very action taken to solve a problem leads to a worsening of the problem over the long term.

 ## MANAGING "FIXES THAT FAIL"

The best way to manage "Fixes That Fail" is to avoid getting into the situation in the first place. For example, when addressing a new problem, take time to think through the nature of the problem. Ask yourself, "How could the solution we want to implement possibly come around and worsen the problem?" Then inquire carefully into the problem *behind* the symptom, clarify the thinking behind proposed solutions, diagram potential unintended consequences, and prepare to manage both short-term and long-term outcomes of your actions. *If it is not possible to fully avoid the longer term difficulties, then it is crucial that you anticipate and prepare for them.*

To turn around an existing "Fixes That Fail" dynamic, first acknowledge that the quick fix is not solving the problem; it's merely alleviating a symptom. Then commit to solving the real problem *now*. Realistically, you may have to continue to apply the immediate fix while simultaneously working out a plan for a more fundamental solution.

Here are some guidelines for getting off the quick-fix treadmill:[2]

- **Define the problem symptom.**

It is easy to confuse solutions with symptoms and make statements such as "The problem is: We need more cash" or "The problem is: We need to expedite this order." Take time to clarify the problem *apart from any actions taken to solve it.* Try turning problem-solution statements such as "lack of cash" or "need to expedite" into problem-*symptom* statements that suggest variables you can graph—for example, "declining working capital" or "increasing customer demand for special handling." Then, in a spirit of investigation rather than blame, ask what is driving that symptom. It might be something like "increasing complexity of small business demand" or "increasing inability to meet customer order deadlines." Responding to these kinds of deeper issues will be far more effective than simply performing a quick fix such as expediting orders.

- **Examine past "solutions" to the problem as well as current and planned ones.**

Be sure to include typical favorites such as training, running promotions, downsizing, or special processing of orders. With each "solution," draw out how you and others believe the fix will rectify the problem. In other words, clarify your mental models. Remember to take this step in a spirit of inquiry and collaboration. By clearly articulating how your solutions affect the original problem, you create an explicit map of your assumptions. Then share your understanding of the problem with others, and invite them to add to or modify the reasoning from their point of view.

- **Map unintended consequences.**

We're usually good at recognizing the *intended* results of our own actions, but not so good at identifying the unintended ones. Sharing your thinking process with others, inviting them to contribute their insights, and role playing so as to put yourself in someone else's "shoes" mentally can help you see beyond your own blind spot.

- **Identify the dynamics that create the problem symptoms.**

Treating symptoms can become a full-time job, because each "fix" creates new symptoms that demand to be "solved." To stop the treadmill, it's essential to identify what is causing the problem in the first place. This is the process you may have begun in the guidelines above. As you may have seen, the search for the fundamental cause can lead to very different questions than you may have anticipated.

- **Look for connections between the unintended consequences and the fundamental causes of the problem symptom.**

Often these two are linked together in ways that further reinforce the continued use of the "fixes." Identifying these links can highlight how the fixes become entrenched in your organization's routines. For example, the entrepreneur's short-term borrowing becomes a habit because it works in the short term.

- **Identify high-leverage interventions.**

High-leverage interventions are structural changes you can make to the system with minimal initial effort or investment that will eventually resolve the fundamental problem. For example, in the entrepreneur story, a fundamental problem was the lack of capital at the start. The entrepreneur scraped enough cash together, when perhaps he should have taken out a sizeable, long-term loan or acquired venture capital to ensure that he had enough working capital to cover the usual start-up costs.

- **Map the potential side-effects of any proposed interventions.**

Anticipating undesirable outcomes lets you better prepare to respond or perhaps even design around these outcomes altogether.

- **Cultivate joint understanding of this archetype.**

Mutual understanding of this archetype can be a powerful tool for legitimizing consideration of longer term, often "softer" consequences (such as morale or enthusiasm) that are real and important parts of the system. Such impacts are often considered undiscussable because, in our hard-nosed, results-oriented world, they are often considered either too "fuzzy" or too uncertain to merit serious attention.

 In Summary

A key point to keep in mind about "Fixes That Fail" is that the problem symptom/quick fix/unintended consequence reinforcing process receives its energy directly from implementation of the quick fix. Every time the quick fix is applied, the unintended-consequence loop is activated again. The faster the quick-fix loop cycles, the more often the unintended-consequence loop is activated. The more energy, effort, and attention that go into the quick-fix cycle, the more these things flow into the unintended-consequences cycle.

It's probably impossible to completely avoid "Fixes That Fail," because we can rarely know all the unintended consequences of our actions. However, to manage this common archetype, we can examine our theories about where a problem comes from and how the solutions will work. Ask yourself, "What is the fundamental problem here?" and "What are the unintended side-effects of my actions?" Inviting input from others can also enhance your thinking and learning.

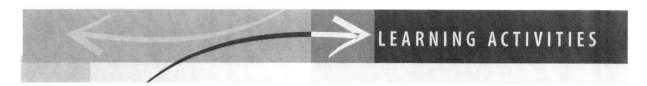

Now that you've learned about "Fixes That Fail," try your hand at the Learning Activities below. These exercises will give you an opportunity to identify "Fixes That Fail" dynamics in stories, and to analyze a "Fixes That Fail" story from your own experience.

In each Learning Activity, you will be asked to provide:

- A statement of the theme of the story

- A list of key variables

- A graph of the key variables' distinctive behavior over time

- A causal loop diagram of the systemic structure generating the "Fixes That Fail" scenario.

After completing the Learning Activities below, compare your responses with those in Appendix A. Don't worry if your responses look different from the ones in the appendix; there's no one right "answer" in a systems thinking analysis. These activities are mainly meant to get you thinking about the themes, patterns of behavior, and systemic structure of the archetypes.

Activity 1   THE DANGERS OF DOWNSIZING

The Story ➤ FutureTech, a large, high-tech company with a specialized market niche, begins to experience financial pressures. Revenues are dropping, and profits are down. After much discussion in the executive committee, it seems as if the financially sound approach is to reduce costs by having a layoff. According to the committee's thinking, reducing the number of service and administrative staff will reduce the overhead of personnel costs, which will in turn increase profits. During the first quarter following the layoff, there *is* a drop in costs, and profit numbers improve.

In the following quarter, profits take another dip. With great regret, the executive committee concludes that they hadn't trimmed enough before, and they mandate another layoff. After a slightly chaotic quarter of adjustment, FutureTech once again sees an improvement in profit figures.

When the executives spot yet another, slightly sharper drop in profits, they decide to investigate before pursuing further cost-cutting measures. They discover that, with fewer service and administrative staff, customer inquiries, billing, and fulfillment materials are being handled more slowly. Service quality has declined, and with it, customers' overall perceptions of the company's product quality. As a result, customers are reluctant to buy, and sales and service revenue have decreased.

INSTRUCTIONS

1. Summarize the "Fixes That Fail" theme in this story in two or three sentences.

2. Identify the key variables in the story. (Remember that variables are things—tangible or intangible—that change over time.) (Variables in brackets below appear in the story but do not have to appear in your causal loop diagram.)

   The problem symptom is that _____ are falling.

   The quick fix is to institute or continue _____, thus reducing [_____.]

   The theory is that the quick fix will bring down _____.

   In actuality, the quick fix also reduces [_____], which brings down

   _____ and [_____].

   _____ fall, which worsens the problem symptom.

3. Graph the behavior over time of the problem symptom, and show the effect of the quick fix on the graph.

4. Using the blank systems archetype template provided, fill in the diagram with the story's key variables. As you develop your diagram, label all the arrows in it with an "s" or an "o" to indicate a change in the "same" or "opposite" direction. Also, be sure to add any important delays. (**Note:** In each section, we've provided these templates in the Learning Activities as one way for you to start diagramming the stories. You may also want to use blank sheets of paper to give yourself more room to try different variables or to add extra variables. Another useful technique, developed by Rick Karash at Innovation Associates, is to use small Post-it™ notes to move variable names around on your diagram.)

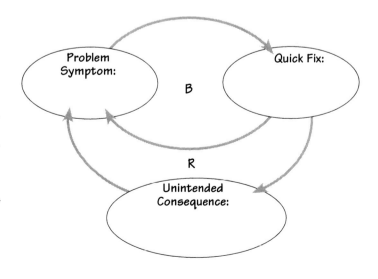

ACTIVITY 2   THE PROBLEM WITH PROMOTIONS

The Story ➤ Games, Inc., a fast-moving consumer electronics company, is experiencing increasing revenue pressures. "Gotta sell, gotta sell. Gotta get more boxes out the door," urges Felix, the sales manager. The marketing department responds by running more promotions: "Free CDs with every player!" "Extra game cartridges with your NEW game box!"

Customers gobble up the promotions. But when the marketing campaigns end, sales fall off and revenue pressure goes up again. "Fire the marketing manager!" the CEO hollers. "Get me someone who can run a really good promotion—one that sticks!"

Then, one Saturday morning, while Felix is standing at the check-out counter in Electronics City with his son, he overhears two adolescents talking about Games, Inc.'s products. "Nah, I don't get that game box," one of the teens says. "They're always giving stuff away. Can't be a good product. Now PowerPlayer, that's awesome—it's so good they don't have to give away nothin'."

INSTRUCTIONS

1. Summarize the "Fixes That Fail" theme in this story in two or three sentences.

2. Identify the key variables in the story.

   Problem symptom:

   Quick fix:

   Quick-fix result that will relieve the problem symptom:

   Unintended consequence of the quick fix (name one or two):

3. Graph the behavior of the problem symptom and the effect of the quick fix.

4. Using the blank systems archetype template below, fill in the diagram with the variables you identified. Feel free to add variables in either loop. Label each arrow with an "s" or an "o" to show "same" or "opposite" direction. Show any important delays.

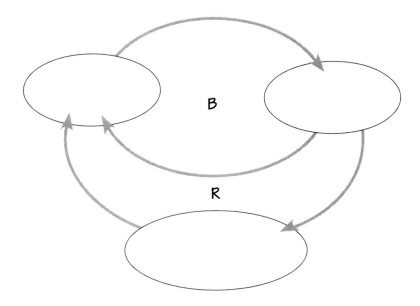

ACTIVITY 3   CAR LEASES THAT FAIL[3]

The Story ➤ In the highly competitive auto industry, car manufacturers are under continual pressure to create more attractive deals so they can maintain profits. A current trend is to offer more aggressive, cut-rate leases on new cars, which help the auto companies in the short term by pumping up unit sales and bringing in more revenue. The long-term side-effects of "too good to be true" leases, however, are slowly beginning to emerge.

One problem is the residual value of the leased cars. Residual value is the car's anticipated wholesale value at the end of the lease. It is set when the company writes the lease. This process presents no inherent problems to the car maker's bottom line, as long as the actual market value of the used car equals its anticipated residual value at the end of the lease. Unfortunately, the actual market price has been falling short of the expectations set during aggressive leasing campaigns—which means losses for car makers when it comes time to sell the previously leased cars. One example cited by a leading business publication is a Japanese car maker's luxury brand. According to the periodical, this car maker set an aggressive, unrealistically high three-year residual on its top-of-the-line model. When the cars began coming off lease, dealers had to sell them at losses ranging from $5,000 to $7,000 apiece.

INSTRUCTIONS

1. Summarize the "Fixes That Fail" theme in this story in two or three sentences.

2. Identify the key variables in the story.

   Problem symptom:

   Quick fix:

   Quick-fix results that will relieve the problem symptom:

   Unintended consequence(s) of the quick fix:

3. Graph the behavior of the problem symptom and the effect of the quick fix.

4. Using the blank systems archetype template below, fill in the diagram with the variables you identified. You may have additional variables in either loop.

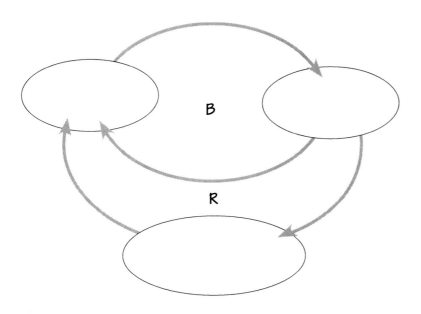

ACTIVITY 4 YOUR OWN FIX THAT FAILS

INSTRUCTIONS

Follow the steps below.

STEP 1: Think of a recurring problem symptom from your work, home, community, or elsewhere—a problem that has some history so you can see actual trends and the impact of actual interventions. Briefly describe the problem symptom below.

STEP 2: Make some notes about the story, enough to remind yourself of what has been happening.

STEP 3: Summarize the story in a couple of sentences. (You may find it is easier to come back to this step after you have worked with the variables and the loop diagram.)

STEP 4: List the key variables in the story. If your initial list is quite long (more than six or seven variables), try aggregating some of them. (For example, "Sales," "Income," and "Profits" might all go under one variable name, "Financial Results.") Or, you can consider narrowing the focus of the story.

Problem symptom:

Quick fix:

Intended consequence(s):

Unintended consequence(s):

STEP 5: Draw the pattern of behavior over time of the problem symptom. Show the impact of the quick fixes.

To confirm your graph, check with colleagues, friends, or family members to see whether your memory of the pattern of behavior matches theirs. *The key to identifying a "Fixes That Fail" dynamic is to notice when the problem symptom persists and possibly worsens in spite of repeated attempts to "solve" it.*

STEP 6: Using the "Fixes That Fail" causal loop template, diagram your situation. Add any extra key variables you wish to either the quick-fix or the unintended-consequences loop. Label each arrow with an "s" or an "o," and label each loop with a "B" or an "R."

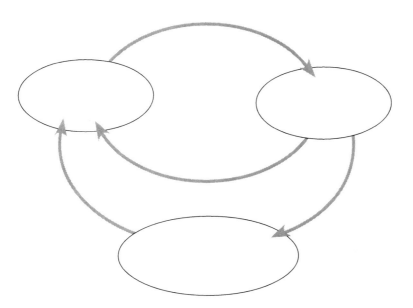

      To confirm the usefulness of your diagram, walk through the logic of both loops. In what sense does the quick-fix loop represent expected short-term effects? Did the expected result happen in the short run, at least to some extent? In what sense does the unintended-consequences loop represent an undesirable, long-term impact? What data or behavior did you see that verifies this?

      You can further check your diagram by asking whether the quick fix actually contributed to maintaining or worsening the problem symptom.

      Finally, validate and broaden your insight by showing your diagram to a friend, colleague, or family member. Remember to position it as your "first-draft" attempt to understand the problem. Explain your diagram in terms of the theory behind the fix and the unintended side-effect of the solution. Then ask what he or she thinks and whether your explanation makes sense. Don't worry if your versions are different. Everyone's version of a story is a unique mental model, and the point is to learn which mental models are at work in the problems facing us.

Notes

1. This section is adapted from "Fixes That Fail: Oiling the Squeaky Wheel—Again and Again," *Systems Archetypes I: Diagnosing Systemic Issues and Designing High-Leverage Interventions,* by Daniel H. Kim (Pegasus Communications, Inc., 1992).
2. Adapted from "Using 'Fixes That Fail' to Get Off the Problem-Solving Treadmill," *Systems Archetypes II: Using Systems Archetypes to Take Effective Action,* by Daniel H. Kim (Pegasus Communications, Inc., 1994).
3. From "Car Leasing: Are Automakers Gambling Away Their Future?" by Kellie T. Wardman, *The Systems Thinker,* Volume 6, Number 2, March 1995 (Pegasus Communications, Inc.).

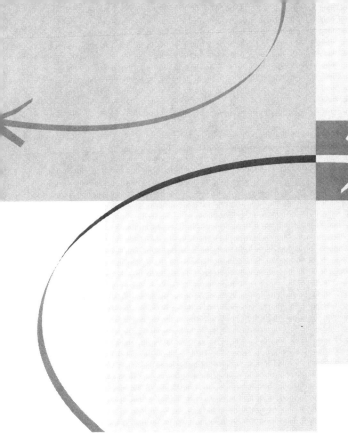

Shifting the Burden

In a "Shifting the Burden" situation, a problem symptom can be addressed by applying a symptomatic solution or a more fundamental solution. When a symptomatic solution is implemented, the problem symptom is reduced or disappears, which lessens the pressure for implementing a more fundamental solution. Over time, the symptom resurfaces, and another round of symptomatic solutions is implemented in a vicious, figure-8 reinforcing cycle. The symptomatic solutions often produce side-effects that further divert attention away from more fundamental solutions.

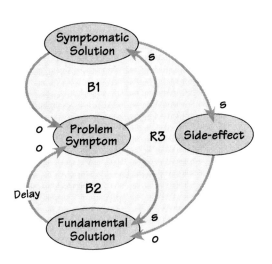

THE STORYLINE:

Too Busy to Run the Scanner?

Everyone at Sawyer, Goodley, and Burns Architecture Associates is delighted when the new blueprint scanner is installed. The intern drafting assistant, Marty, had learned how to use one in graduate school, and he promises to teach all the architects how it works. Two days later, at 5:30 p.m., Karen Sawyer needs to express-mail reduced prints to a client. "Marty, I want to learn how to use this machine, but I need to get these prints out right now," she says. "Could you produce the reductions on the 664 Main Street project for me?" The following week, in the middle of a meeting, Neal Burns rushes to Marty's

25

work table. "Marty," he pants, "is there any way that machine could make an overhead of the original layout we had for the first floor of the Ballard building? Kirchoffer and his boss are looking for alternative approaches. Oh . . . yeah, maybe next week you can show me how it works."

Over the next six months, the blueprint scanner is used more and more frequently—by Marty. First Marty begins to joke that he has become the intern scanning assistant. Then he half-kiddingly threatens to charge each architect per page. Finally, he begins to remind them that his internship will be ending at Christmas, and even though the holiday season is busy, they'd better take the time to learn to use the scanner themselves. But as the holiday months approach, no one makes a move to familiarize themselves with the machine.

 ## "SHIFTING THE BURDEN" TO THE CENTRAL OFFICE EXPERTS

Here's the same sort of storyline, but in a completely different company: A claims office in a local branch of Southeast Mutual, a large insurance company, is faced with a large, complex claim that requires more expertise than it possesses. The company's central office responds by sending out its team of expert investigators and adjusters to take care of the situation while the branch office staff goes about their more routine business. Everyone agrees that the company cannot justify having teams of experts in every branch, given the cost and the fact that these complicated claims occur so infrequently.

Besides, everyone knows that people who want to get involved with complex, technically challenging claims either have to move to Southeast's central office or work locally for a different company. Gradually, the most talented people take those options, and it becomes more difficult to replace them with equally capable adjusters. The branch office begins to rely more and more on the support of the central office. In fact, as the central office expert team grows increasingly efficient at handling crises around the region, the branch seeks their help more and more often as the number of claims that cannot be handled locally increases.

 ## THE "HELEN KELLER" LOOPS: THE GENERIC STORY BEHIND "SHIFTING THE BURDEN"[1]

The basic storyline in "Shifting the Burden" has been compared to the story of Helen Keller, the blind and deaf child whose parents' attempts to protect her only made her dependent on them. Even though Helen's parents were well intentioned, they shifted the burden of responsibility for Helen's welfare to *themselves*. Helen learned that no matter what she did, her parents would accommodate her. And each incident reinforced her parents' belief that she was indeed helpless. If it had not been for the determined efforts of Helen's teacher, Ann Sullivan, who refused to let Helen's handicaps prevent her from becoming self-reliant, Helen may never have achieved her real potential.

As with "Fixes That Fail," "Shifting the Burden" is about how the pressure of a worsening problem can lead us to institute a quick fix. In this case, we resort increasingly to a quick, symptomatic solution rather than work out a more fundamental solution that is often more difficult to implement. Also similar to "Fixes That Fail," the relatively quick symptomatic fix often sets off hard-to-detect, unintended side-effects that frequently undermine our efforts to implement a fundamental solution and that can even accentuate the original problem.

SYMPTOMATIC AND FUNDAMENTAL SOLUTIONS: BEHAVIOR OVER TIME

FIGURE 3.1

Behavior Over Time of Symptomatic and Fundamental Solutions

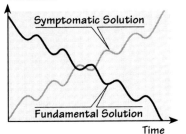

With a "Shifting the Burden" structure, a graph of the symptomatic and fundamental solutions' behavior over time typically shows an "X" pattern (see Figure 3.1, "Behavior Over Time of Symptomatic and Fundamental Solutions"). The line indicating the application of the quick fix or symptomatic solution rises in a wavering pattern that reflects the intermittent impact of that activity. The line indicating the application of (or attention to) the fundamental solution usually drops, sometimes in a smooth line (if there is no attention given to it) and sometimes in a wavering line if it is applied intermittently and less and less frequently.

THE SYSTEMIC STRUCTURE BEHIND "SHIFTING THE BURDEN"

"Shifting the Burden" usually begins with a *problem symptom* that prompts us to intervene and "solve" it. We apply a symptomatic solution that does ease the problem symptom for a time (B1 in Figure 3.2, "The Structure Behind 'Shifting the Burden,'" p. 28). After we apply the symptomatic solution, the problem symptom eases, and we feel no need to adopt the more difficult, time-consuming fundamental solution. The symptomatic solution also has a side-effect that contributes to the erosion of our ability to implement a fundamental solution. Though it usually takes more time and effort, that fundamental solution is more likely to solve the problem at the root-cause level and keep the problem symptom from recurring (B2). Unfortunately, with each application of the symptomatic solution, the impact of the side-effect becomes greater and greater through a reinforcing process, and our ability to implement a fundamental solution spirals downward faster and faster (R3).

FIGURE 3.2

The Structure Behind "Shifting the Burden"

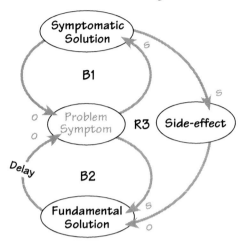

  APPLYING STRUCTURE TO STORY

Let's see how the stories about Sawyer, Goodley, and Burns, and Southeast Mutual would look mapped onto the generic "Shifting the Burden" systemic structure. In the case of the architects' office (see the causal loop diagram in Figure 3.3, "Shifting the Burden to Marty"), the problem symptom is the need to use the blueprint scanner under time pressure. The quick fix or symptomatic solution is to get Marty to run the scanner (B4).

But symptomatic solutions have two undesirable impacts. First, because they solve the problem in the short run, they divert attention away from the real (or fundamental) source of the problem, which in this case is the need for scanner training for the staff (B5). More subtly, the

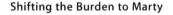

FIGURE 3.3

Shifting the Burden to Marty

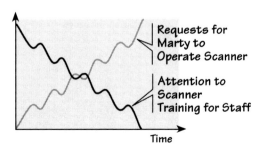

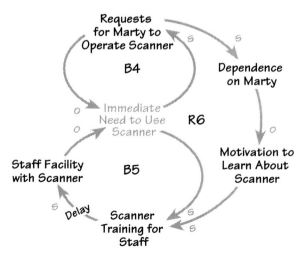

symptomatic solution's side-effect—whereby the dependence on Marty increases and the motivation to learn about the scanner decreases—further erodes the viability of the fundamental solution over time (R6). As motivation to learn about the scanner decreases, so do efforts to train the staff to use the scanner. The dwindling attention given to the fundamental solution intensifies the need for the symptomatic fix, so the participants in the system rely more and more on the short-term fix. At Sawyer, Goodley, and Burns, the more the associates asked Marty to run the scanner for them, the more dependent they grew on him and the less motivated they were to train themselves to use the machine. Because Marty was fulfilling their short-term needs, the idea of learning to use the scanner themselves seemed less and less important. This fundamental solution would have taken more time, anyway, and might have temporarily put more stress and pressure on people as they tried to use the scanner to service clients immediately. It just seemed easier and easier to keep asking Marty to help.

The pattern of behavior that the architects fell into is easy to understand, and quite widespread. With all our best intentions to learn to use a new machine or show the rest of our department how to use a new piece of software, we continue to do whatever relieves the pressure on us right away. The consequences of going with the symptomatic solution may be minor: Sawyer, Goodley, Burns will have to pay Marty to return for a morning to teach them how to use the scanner, or the associates will have to struggle on their own to learn from the scanner instruction book.

But "Shifting the Burden" can have a more dramatic effect when it functions on a larger scale, which is what happened at Southeast Mutual. At Southeast, the problem symptom was the pressure to process complex claims outside the experience of the branch adjusters (see Figure 3.4, "Shifting the Burden to the Central Office"). The symptomatic solution was to ask the central office to process the complex claims (B7). One possible fundamental solution was to strengthen the local branch's ability to

FIGURE 3.4

Shifting the Burden to the Central Office

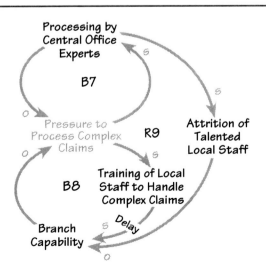

handle at least some larger, more complex claims. True, this solution would have required an investment of management attention, expertise, training, and time, both for learning and practice. But it also would have led to learning on the part of the local staff, and would have strengthened the branch office's overall capability and its ability to underwrite more business. An additional price of that investment might include an initial reduction in the quality of claims settlements as local staff made some mistakes while coming up the learning curve—the common "worse before better" characteristic of fundamental change in complex systems.

Instead, the local branches relied more and more on the central office to process the difficult claims. This symptomatic solution had several undesirable, unintended consequences, one of which was a gradual centralization of the entire company. The more the branch offices relied on the central office, the more knowledge and resources became concentrated in areas away from the branch offices. In addition, talented employees—whether potential or existing—began to see career possibilities as available primarily at the central office rather than the local branches (R9).

Although there may have been nothing necessarily wrong with a centralized organizational structure at Southeast, it did carry several dangers. First, centralization could have become a short-term, easy way out of solving difficult problems. Furthermore, the shift of expertise away from branch offices might have been dangerous because it didn't involve strategic forethought and long-term vision. Finally, centralization at Southeast had another important consequence: The central office team felt more and more pressure as they became overloaded, and customers drifted away because of the team's slow response and the branch offices' inability to respond more locally.

But let's go back to the fundamental solution: enhancing local adjusters' expertise with complex claims. Resorting to central office experts had two side-effects that weakened Southeast's inclination to implement this more permanent solution. First, the branch offices' expectation that the central office would intervene grew. Second, as that expectation was met, the technically proficient employees increasingly migrated to the central office or to outside firms, and the branch lost its pool of talented adjusters (R9).

 ## DIAGRAMMING "SHIFTING THE BURDEN"

As in "Fixes That Fail," one of the first signals that a "Shifting the Burden" structure is at work is a problem symptom that keeps coming back and an inclination to apply an immediate, easy solution that relieves the pressure right away. Another important signal is the suspicion or realization that a more effective response to the problem exists, but that this response would require much time, investment, commitment, or change. A third clue is problem-solving behavior that seems compulsive or addictive; this quality suggests an increasing reliance on the symptomatic solution.

To start diagramming a structure that you suspect is a case of "Shifting the Burden," it's often easiest to identify the problem symptom and the quick symptomatic fix—the upper balancing loop of the diagram. When you graph these two variables, you'll see a recurring pattern of the problem intensifying, then the fix being implemented, and the problem diminishing, only to be repeated.

Once you've drawn the upper balancing loop demonstrating how the quick fix brings the problem symptom back under control, identify a more fundamental solution that would also bring the problem symptom under control, but usually in a longer timeframe. Finally, try to identify any side-effects that might further weaken the ability to implement the more fundamental solution.

 ## A DEEPER LOOK AT "SHIFTING THE BURDEN"

The structure of "Shifting the Burden" is an expansion of "Fixes That Fail." It starts with a *balancing* dynamic, in which the magnitude of a problem reaches an intolerable level and pushes us to resort to a symptomatic solution. This solution works—for a time. Because the immediate solution is effective in such a visible way, we may even disagree within our organization about whether it is in fact a "symptomatic" solution or a "fundamental" one.

In a "Shifting the Burden" situation, it's important not to frame the fundamental solution as the "right" solution, because "rightness" often depends on one's perspective. Instead, when trying to distinguish between symptomatic and fundamental solutions, ask whose perspective is under consideration, and examine the problem from multiple viewpoints so as to get a better understanding of the structure and a potential solution.

Side-effects in "Shifting the Burden" can also be hard to detect or acknowledge in an organization. The side-effects' reinforcing process has an especially insidious result: The more frequently or insistently the quick fix is applied, the more energy that goes into the reinforcing process that undermines investments in a more fundamental solution.

"Shifting the Burden" has several intriguing variations. At Southeast Mutual, the organization experienced the variation known as "Shifting the Burden to the Intervener." In this variation, an individual or group in need of help depends on an expert intervener. Over time, dependency on the intervener increases.

The more extreme form of "Shifting the Burden to the Intervener" is the "Addiction" structure, which usually occurs when people are in pain or distress and under pressure, and are desperately searching for relief. A symptomatic solution, such as using drugs or alcohol to cope with stress, looks like a simple answer in the moment—it is very seductive, especially under conditions of despair. In organizations, addiction can take many forms, including dependence on certain policies, procedures, cultural norms, departments, or individuals. These dependencies can become addictions when we use them without consideration or choice; that is, as a "knee-jerk" reaction to pressures. "Shifting the Burden to the Intervener" can be addictive in its own way—we shift responsibility to someone else, their intervention becomes the easy way out when pressure builds up, and eventually we grow dependent on them, unable to respond to the problem on our own.

MANAGING "SHIFTING THE BURDEN"

The best way to manage a "Shifting the Burden" situation is to avoid it completely, or, if that's not possible, to prevent it from becoming entrenched. As with "Fixes That Fail," it helps to pay attention to the pressures that push us into responding automatically rather than thoughtfully. It's also important to notice when we are responding primarily to relieve *pressure* rather than to address a *problem*. Finally, noticing problems that seem to recur in spite of attempts to solve them can tip us off to an impending "Shifting the Burden" situation. Here are some guidelines for handling this particularly stubborn archetype:

- **Ask questions.**

If you notice that you or your organization are responding to a problem with a quick fix, ask yourself the following questions:

"What is the deeper cause of this problem?"

"Is there something we would like to do about this problem if we just had time, money, energy, approval, or other resources?"

"Is the current solution congruent with our larger vision? If not, what approach would be congruent?"

"What are the possible long-term consequences of using this solution? The possible unintended side-effects?"

- **Commit to work on the fundamental solution even if you have to keep using the symptomatic solution for the time being.**

It's a fact of life that the quick fix meets a need; it's probably unwise to stop using it overnight. After all, someone needs to run the blueprint scanner, handle the complex claims, or juggle project crises *today*. The way to get out of the "Shifting the Burden" structure usually involves continuing to support the quick fix, but at the same time, instituting or reviving the more fundamental solution as well. The key is that as the fundamental solution begins to take effect, you must taper off use of the symptomatic quick fix.

- **Stay focused on your organization's vision.**

"Shifting the Burden" often comes into play when the primary goal has become relieving discomfort or pressure and feeling better. In addition, the quick fix becomes especially attractive when a company shifts its emphasis to the short term. Avoiding or turning around a "Shifting the Burden" structure requires balancing the short and long term.

- **Keep an eye out for the Addiction version of "Shifting the Burden."**

To identify the Addiction dynamic at work, use the "Shifting the Burden" archetype as a diagnostic tool and ask questions such as, "What is the addiction responding to?" "Why do we feel a need to engage in this behavior or create this dependency in the first place?" and "What are the problem symptoms that we are responding to?"

Addiction structures can be much more difficult to reverse than the garden-variety "Shifting the Burden" because they tend to be more deeply ingrained. Just as you cannot cure alcoholism by simply removing the alcohol, you cannot attempt a frontal assault on an organizational addiction, because it is firmly rooted in many other dynamics of the organization. If your organization is addicted to fire fighting, for example, declaring a ban on heroics may be the worst thing you can do. If heroics is the only way your organization knows how to release the accumulated pressures produced by ineffective processes, ending that practice might actually provoke an explosion or systemic breakdown. Instead, explore what it is about the system that creates crises and leaves fire fighting as the only option for handling them. It may be that the lure of rewards for putting out fires actually motivates people to *create* fires to be put out, perhaps as a subconscious rejection of fundamental solutions!

IN SUMMARY

"Shifting the Burden" highlights an all-too-common human tendency to eliminate feelings of discomfort or pain as quickly as possible. This tendency usually leads us down the path of focusing on symptoms rather than on more fundamental causes. This archetype also reveals how easy it is to become addicted to such symptomatic solutions, even as we become less and less willing or able to invest in a more fundamental solution.

But like the other systems archetypes, "Shifting the Burden" can also help you uncover many different potential solutions to problems, as well as deepen your understanding of the system in which the problems unfold. With most problems in life, there is never just one fundamental solution. By using this archetype, you can map out several short- and long-term solutions, and explore the role of the symptomatic solution's side-effect on various possible fundamental solutions. "Shifting the Burden" encourages you to look beyond actions taken merely to relieve immediate pressure, and even to consider how you may be unconsciously resisting a more effective solution and becoming "hooked on" a habitual response.

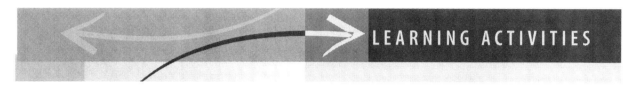

Now that you've learned about "Shifting the Burden," try your hand at the Learning Activities below. These exercises will give you an opportunity to identify "Shifting the Burden" dynamics in case studies, and to analyze a "Shifting the Burden" story from your own experience.

In each Learning Activity, you will be asked to provide:

- A statement of the theme of the story
- A list of key variables
- A graph of the key variables' distinctive behavior over time
- A causal loop diagram of the systemic structure generating the "Shifting the Burden" situation.

After completing the Learning Activities below, compare your responses with those in Appendix A. Don't worry if your responses look different from the ones in the appendix; there's no one right "answer" in a systems thinking analysis. These activities are mainly meant to get you thinking about the themes, patterns of behavior, and systemic structure of the archetypes.

ACTIVITY 1   PRICE PROMOTIONS: WHAT ARE THEY REALLY PUSHING?[2]

The Story ➤ As U.S. population growth has slowed, major consumer goods manufacturers have experienced a slowdown in sales growth for many of their products. In the view of some of these companies, they have been dragged into the middle of an all-out campaign for control of consumer goods prices, market share, and profits. Because of a lack of real product innovations, manufacturers are often unable to distinguish their brands in meaningful ways other than through price. Hence, they have resorted to continual price promotion campaigns.

Industry analysts have pointed out that these price promotion campaigns carry some unwanted side-effects. For one thing, promotions can erode brand image and encourage consumers to shop solely on price. Also, manufacturers and retailers themselves can become "hooked" on short-term promotions to continue pumping up sales numbers.

The long-term implications are even more disturbing. Manufacturers' dependence on promotions has given supermarkets great power, because they ultimately control promotions. They can demand a wide range of subsidies from manufacturers. This means that a large percentage of discounts intended for consumers wind up in retailers' pockets, and that funds for improvements in brand image and quality are diverted to even more price promotions. The need for a higher leverage solution has never been more important.

INSTRUCTIONS

1. Summarize the "Shifting the Burden" theme in this story in two or three sentences.

2. Identify the key variables in the story.

   The problem symptom is that _____ are falling.

   The quick fix is to institute or continue _____.

   A more fundamental solution is to invest in _____.

   The quick fix also increases _____, which cut into _____,
   and thus undermine manufacturers' ability to support the more fundamental solution.

3. Graph the behavior over time of the symptomatic solution and the fundamental solution.

4. Fill in the blank systems archetype template with the variables you identified above. Feel free to add extra variables to any loop in the template. Be sure to label each arrow in your diagram with an "s" or "o," to show "same" or "opposite" change, and show any important delays.

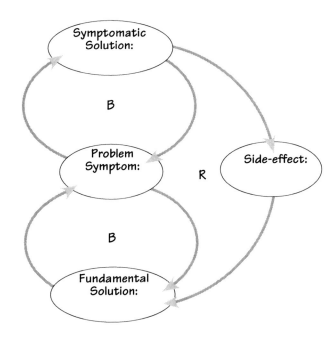

ACTIVITY 2   **ADDICTION TO BLAME**

The Story ➤ When something goes wrong at ABCo Rentals and the stress is on, the first question the employees often ask is, "Whose fault is it?" When there's data missing in accounting, it's the bookkeeper's fault. If ABCo loses a key customer, it's the sales group's problem—"They promised more than we could deliver!" When errors such as these surface, blaming seems to be a natural reflex. Even those individuals who sincerely want to learn from mistakes give in to the temptation to name culprits.

Pat Wiley, an OD consultant working with ABCo, has noticed that, when the blaming starts, open minds close up, inquiry stops, and the desire to understand how the whole system is involved diminishes. Pat's interviews with employees reveal a common theme at ABCo: It's safer to cover up errors and hide real concerns than bring them into the open. Some people suspect that, because of this characteristic of ABCo's culture, they're missing out on valuable information that could lead to improved policies and procedures. However, no one has the courage to try to change things.

Working with the management team, Pat encourages them to clarify accountability by focusing on tasks, roles, processes, standards, and expected results—not on individual personalities and competencies. Each group is planning to set up meetings to review their progress on this change work.

INSTRUCTIONS

1. Summarize the "Shifting the Burden" theme in this story in two or three sentences.

2. Identify the key variables in the story.

Problem symptom:

Symptomatic solution:

Side-effect of symptomatic solution:

More fundamental solution:

3. Graph the behavior over time of the symptomatic solution and the fundamental solution.

4. Using the blank systems archetype template, fill in the diagram with the variables you identified. Feel free to add variables or loops. Label each arrow with an "s" or an "o," and add any important delays.

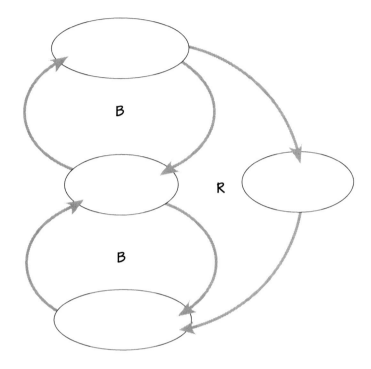

ACTIVITY 3 — SHIFTING AUTHORITY THROUGH EMPOWERMENT[3]

The Story ➤ As hotels struggle to remain competitive in today's tough market, many are being forced to make changes in their management structure to improve responsiveness to guests. Over the last few years, the ratio of hotel employees to rooms has decreased. With fewer managers around, many day-to-day hotel decisions are now being delegated to direct service employees. With this shift in authority, the ability to do whatever it takes to respond to customers extends not only to people at the front desk, but to all hotel employees.

At the upscale Carriage House, management decides to initiate such an empowerment program. Employees can now take the initiative to give away almost anything to ensure customer loyalty—from free terrycloth robes to write-offs of bills for unhappy customers. In one instance, Carriage House pays over $3,000 for clothes, toiletries, and other necessities for a couple whose luggage got lost when a bellman accidentally loaded it into the wrong rental car.

Although employee "empowerment" programs have been valuable in many organizations, the program at Carriage House has created some unexpected difficulties. Often, the only increased problem-solving authority hotel employees have is to respond to customer complaints. When their goal becomes pleasing customers at any cost, the focus is taken away from finding cost-effective and efficient ways to run the hotel, especially if employees receive little or no training regarding appropriate resolutions. In these cases, they have limited understanding of the bottom-line impact of their actions, so their "damage control" leads to high costs.

Furthermore, a gradual erosion in real service quality gets masked by happy customers who have been "bought off," and by employees who presumably perform better as a result of their increased authority. Also, when wages do not increase along with responsibilities, employee resentment grows and eventually jeopardizes the very service quality that empowerment programs are intended to improve.

INSTRUCTIONS

1. Summarize the "Shifting the Burden" theme in this story in two or three sentences.

2. Identify the key variables in the story.

   Problem that employees can address:

   Symptomatic solution:

   More fundamental solution:

   Unintended side-effects that undermine the fundamental solution:

3. Graph the behavior of the symptomatic solution in relation to the fundamental solution.

4. Using the blank systems archetype template, fill in the diagram with the variables you identified. You may want to add additional variables or loops. Label each arrow with an "s" or an "o" and mark any important delays. Label each loop with an "R" or a "B" for "reinforcing" and "balancing."

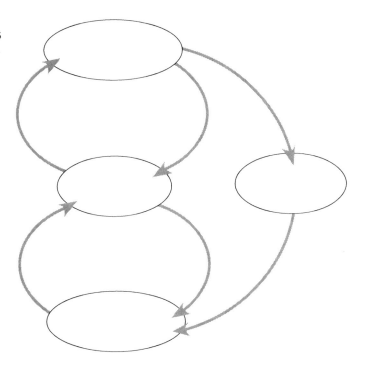

ACTIVITY 4   **YOUR OWN CASE OF "SHIFTING THE BURDEN"**

INSTRUCTIONS

Follow the steps below.

STEP 1: Think of a problem from work, home, community, or elsewhere that you suspect might be a "Shifting the Burden" situation. Pick a problem that has some history, so you can see actual trends and the impact of actual interventions. Describe the problem briefly below.

STEP 2: Write down some notes about the story, enough to remind yourself of what has been happening.

STEP 3: Summarize the story in a couple of sentences. (You may find it is easier to come back to this step after you have worked with the variables and the loop diagram.)

STEP 4: List the key variables from your story. If your initial list is quite long (more than six or seven variables), try aggregating some of them. Also consider narrowing the focus of the story.

Problem symptom:

Symptomatic solution:

Fundamental solution (may have one or more components):

Unintended side-effect(s):

STEP 5: Draw the pattern of behavior over time of the symptomatic solution in relation to the fundamental solution.

To confirm the usefulness of your graph, check with colleagues, friends, or family members to see whether your memory of the pattern of behavior matches theirs. The key to identifying a "Shifting the Burden" dynamic is noticing that the problem symptom persists, the quick fix continues to be applied, and the fundamental solution (or the capacity to apply it) deteriorates.

STEP 6: Using the "Shifting the Burden" causal loop template, diagram your situation. Add any extra key variables to either the fundamental solution or the unintended-consequences loop as necessary. Label all the arrows and loops.

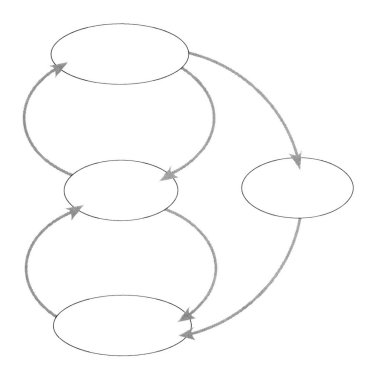

    To confirm the usefulness of your diagram, walk through the logic of the loops. Does the symptomatic solution loop accurately represent what happens when the usual, reliable, immediate solution is applied? Does the fundamental solution loop indicate what it would really take, given a longer-term perspective, to address the original problem at a deeper level? Did you indicate important delays in this loop? What are the implications of those delays? Does the unintended-consequences loop accurately represent an eventual undesirable impact that either worsens the problem or detracts from the fundamental solution?

    Check your diagram further by asking whether the symptomatic solution and its side-effects did actually contribute to maintaining or worsening the problem symptom.

    Finally, validate and broaden your insight by showing your diagram to a friend, colleague, or family member. Engage them in an exploration of ways in which you might break out of this structure and be able to invest in the more fundamental solution. Remember to position it as your "first-draft" attempt to understand what's happening. Explain your diagram in terms of the symptomatic (quick-fix) solution and the fundamental solution ("if we had time, money, etc."). Then ask the person what he or she thinks and whether your explanation makes sense. Don't worry if your versions are different. Everyone's version of the story is a unique mental model, and the point is to learn more about the mental models at work in the problems facing us.

Notes

1. This section is adapted from "'Shifting the Burden': The 'Helen Keller' Loops," *Systems Archetypes I: Diagnosing Systemic Issues and Designing High-Leverage Interventions,* by Daniel H. Kim (Pegasus Communications, Inc., 1992).

2. From "Promotions: What Are They Really Pushing?" by Colleen Lannon, *The Systems Thinker,* Volume 3, Number 3, April 1992 (Pegasus Communications, Inc.).

3. From "Empowerment or 'Shifting the Burden'?" by Anne Coyle, *The Systems Thinker,* Volume 4, Number 4, May 1993 (Pegasus Communications, Inc.).

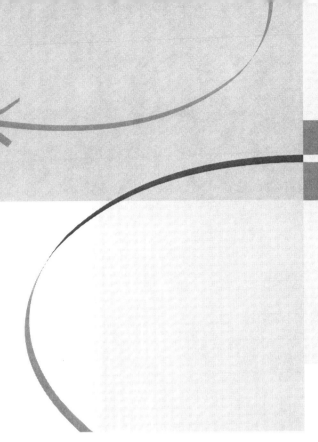

Limits to Success

In a "Limits to Success" scenario, growing actions initially lead to success, which encourages even more of those efforts. Over time, however, the success itself causes the system to encounter limits, which slows down improvements in results. As the success triggers the limiting action and performance declines, the tendency is to focus even more on the initial growing actions.

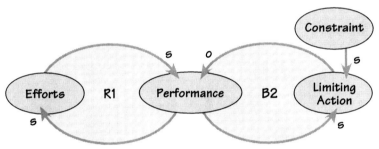

THE STORYLINE:

R&D or Management Development?

Once ImagePhone's first video telephone model is available at an acceptable price and can transmit a recognizable image, the company is off and running. Miriam and Joe, engineering-school buddies and ImagePhone's founding partners, are convinced that the secret to bringing in sales is to maintain investments in R&D. As long as they keep developing technological refinements and innovations to their product line, they'll have a steady stream of new products and accessories to offer. A combination of new products and product enhancements, they believe, will bring in both new and old customers.

"Techies" and gadget lovers snap up ImagePhone products. The company acquires a reputation for producing high-quality products, and customers discover an increasing range of uses for them, from business conferences to remote product displays to family "visits." As ImagePhone adds computer interfaces and wireless technology, sales boom.

43

In the beginning, Miriam had handled marketing and finance, and Joe had worked with manufacturing and shipping. They decide to bring in Scott to manage product innovation. Otherwise, to keep costs down and maintain a focus on R&D, the partners use well-educated staff and contractors and avoid building a large organizational structure.

However, as sales increase and the number of products grows, pressures to restructure the company mount. The partners are running themselves ragged trying to manage strategic and financial planning, marketing, sales-force development, retail relationships, purchasing, human resources, and a half-dozen other functions. The R&D technical staff can no longer field customer inquiries. Product-instruction booklets are either late or inaccurate, and accessories, such as cords, plugs, and mounts, are sometimes missing from product boxes. New products begin to reach retailers late, sometimes by a week or more.

With some outside help, Miriam, Joe, and Scott lay out a design for the company and go out to look for more managers and staff. Unfortunately, they underestimate the delays in finding and training people as well as in communicating their expectations to suppliers and contractors. Several retail outlets cut back on their orders and stop featuring ImagePhone products in their promotions. Products move more slowly. With sales slumping, the management team has no choice but to reduce investment. The company falls behind the competition and eventually goes out of business.

LIMITS TO EMPOWERMENT

In the "Shifting the Burden" section, we encountered the story of empowerment in the hotel industry. Let's take a closer look at this development, to see how this story might also lend itself to the "Limits to Success" theme. As we saw, hotels have cut back on the size of their management teams to contain costs. As a result, direct service staff handling reservations, check-in, luggage, meal service, and other guest services have been given authority to offer extras and even compensation in response to guest requests or complaints. The overriding goal is to create customer loyalty.

How far can hotels go with this effort? Imagine the scenario. Management believes that empowering staff members to exercise local authority to satisfy customers will increase customer loyalty. More loyal customers means more guest nights and more revenue. The success of this empowerment emphasis leads managers to encourage staff to take even more initiative at the local level.

Of course, as staff have more authority to satisfy customers, they gain more experience about what customers really want. This knowledge leads them to recommend other changes in what services are provided and how. They might even begin to insist on more of a voice in how the hotels are run. But what happens when they reach the limits of what hotel management is willing to empower them to do?

Frustration sets in. Staff become discouraged and resentful. Some of them care less about using their authority to satisfy guests; others leave for positions where they can continue to exercise their new-found authority. Returning guests notice the difference first and start booking with the competition. They stop recommending certain hotels to their friends and colleagues. New customers find nothing to differentiate one hotel from any other, and make their next reservations wherever they can get a good room rate. Somehow, things haven't worked out the way anyone planned.

"RAGS-TO-RICHES-TO-RAGS": *THE GENERIC STORY BEHIND "LIMITS TO SUCCESS"*

The generic storyline behind the "Limits to Success" archetype can be compared with a "rags-to-riches-to-rags" story. In the beginning, an individual or organization is focused on growing an enterprise. They work out a way to make this happen—the engine of growth—and set it in motion. For some period of time, it works; the enterprise flourishes.

But when the engine of growth is put in place, one or more other factors are either unknown, ignored, or downplayed. These are the limiting factors, and one or more of them is linked to the engine of growth.

As the engine revs up and the enterprise prospers, the limiting factor is activated, too—but usually after a delay. Eventually, this limiting factor builds up energy and asserts itself. Suddenly, growth slows down. If the limiting factor is not addressed, it can actually reverse the engine of growth into an engine of decline.

The participants in a "Limits to Success" scenario are usually unaware of the two parts of the structure. They see growth or improving performance resulting directly from certain efforts. They are encouraged to continue and even to increase those efforts, and indeed see further improvement. When performance begins to level off, the natural reaction is to increase the same efforts that led to success in the past. But the harder they push, the harder the system seems to push back, as if it had reached some limit or barrier that resists even the most energetic efforts to revive performance.

PLATEAUING PERFORMANCE: *BEHAVIOR OVER TIME IN "LIMITS TO SUCCESS"*

FIGURE 4.1

Performance Over Time in "Limits to Success"

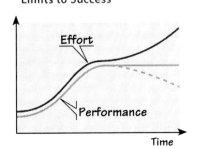

Like the other systems archetypes, "Limits to Success" has its own trademark pattern of behavior over time. With this archetype, the distinctive behavior is exponential growth that eventually either levels off or declines (see Figure 4.1, "Performance Over Time in 'Limits to Success'"). This leveling off or decline forms an s-shaped curve that persists even as efforts are stepped up to revive performance.

THE SYSTEMIC STRUCTURE BEHIND "LIMITS TO SUCCESS"

The "Limits to Success" archetype has a structure characterized by a reinforcing process (which serves as the initial growth engine) and a balancing process (which contains the limits that eventually cause growth to level off) (see Figure 4.2, "The Systemic Structure Behind 'Limits to Success'").

Let's do a quick walk-through of the causal loop diagram: As efforts increase, so does performance, which encourages even more efforts (R1). But the performance (or growth) itself is linked to a limiting factor or action such that, as performance increases, so do the forces slowing the success. The limiting factor then comes back around to *decrease* performance (B2). The key thing to realize with this dynamic is that the reinforcing process dominates during the growth period, until the balancing process becomes dominant as it cuts off further growth potential.

FIGURE 4.2

The Systemic Structure Behind "Limits to Success"

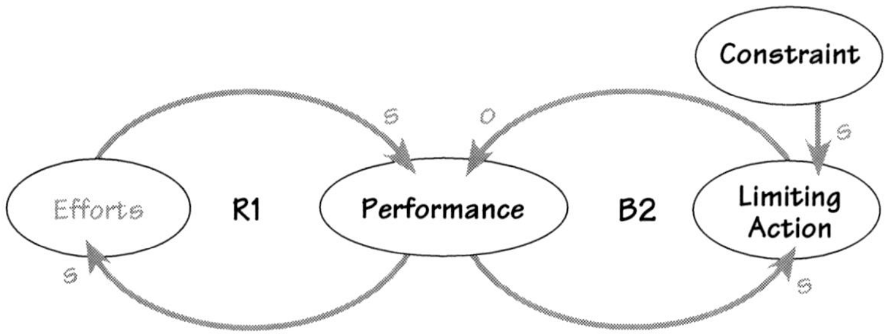

APPLYING STRUCTURE TO STORY

At ImagePhone, the partners believed that R&D and product innovations would drive growth—and for a while the company did grow. The partners didn't feel the need to give much consideration to structuring the organization to respond to its growth, or to hiring managers and staff. Eventually they hit the limit of what they could do without restructuring and hiring. Unfortunately, the delays involved when they finally took those steps resulted in damage to sales and set the company on a dangerous path.

A graph of ImagePhone's sales performance shows their growth, then a leveling off, then a decline (see Figure 4.3, "ImagePhone's Sales Over Time"). In a causal loop diagram of the ImagePhone story (see Figure 4.4, "Limits to ImagePhone's Growth"), management capacity is the constraint that puts a limit on the quality of customer service. As we saw in the story, as sales go up, investment in R&D also rises, leading to new products and accessories, which in turn boost sales (R3). But as sales go up, the growth also increases pressure on management, which reduces the

FIGURE 4.3

ImagePhone's Sales Over Time

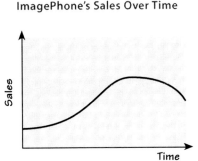

FIGURE 4.4

Limits to ImagePhone's Growth

quality of customer service. As customer service worsens, customer satisfaction decreases, and so do sales (B4).

Similarly, at the hotels, managers believed that giving employees the authority to satisfy guests' requests and complaints would strengthen customer loyalty. Over time, though, there was a limit to how much authority management was willing to grant. The resulting frustration and discouragement undercut staff's use of their authority to please guests, and customer loyalty began to suffer (see Figure 4.5, "The Limits to Empowerment").

As the diagram shows, the initial engine of growth is loop R5, in which an emphasis on empowerment increases the staff's ability to exercise authority at the local level. This allows them to be highly responsive to

FIGURE 4.5

The Limits to Empowerment

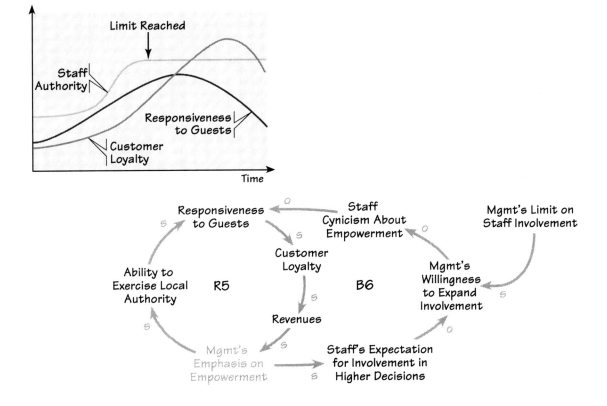

customers' needs, which enhances customer loyalty and revenue. Management, encouraged by the positive results, continues to emphasize empowerment as a key management initiative.

As staff are encouraged to be empowered in making local decisions, however, they begin to see the limits to making changes at just the local level. Because of management's emphasis on empowerment, staff's expectations of becoming more involved in these higher level decisions increase. Initially, management is quite open to the new ideas being suggested for the higher level issues, but after a while, they begin to feel that the staff are really overstepping the bounds and encroaching on management's own jobs. Thus, management's willingness to expand involvement decreases. As staff's cynicism about the sincerity of empowerment grows, their responsiveness to customers declines (B6).

Management responds to this deteriorating situation by renewing their emphasis on empowerment, especially with the new employees who are hired to replace those who have left. However, they find it increasingly more difficult to motivate people to exercise local authority even as they spend more time, money, and effort to "empower" their staff. Through all this, it never occurs to them to examine how their own beliefs about the limit of staff involvement may be undermining their empowerment efforts.

DIAGRAMMING A "LIMITS TO SUCCESS" STRUCTURE

To diagram a "Limits to Success" structure, try using a two-step process. First, draw the engine of growth—the reinforcing process that represents both the initial theory about how to grow the enterprise and the actual mechanism that worked for a while.

Then, to discover the limiting process, ask a series of questions: "What pressures does the growth produce in the system?" "How might those pressures cause a deterioration in performance?" "What capacity limits or bottlenecks do we see?" "How might the growth be pushing some people's mental or emotional limits?"

As you saw in the stories, there is one variable in the growth loop that eventually triggers the action of the limiting loop. You will probably find that you identify this variable through a trial-and-error process, at first. In the ImagePhone story, for example (Figure 4.4), we can assume that the growth mechanism is relatively easy to identify: More R&D leads to more new products, which lead to more sales.

If you know that the limiting factor in ImagePhone's case ultimately was customer service, you can then back up to create the balancing side of the diagram. Which of the growth factors has a connection to customer service? The most likely answer is sales. Common sense (and research at ImagePhone) tells you that the more products that are sold, the more likely it is that eventually customers will have questions, and if a large number of products are sold, there may be a large need for customer service. Filling in the management and structure variables results from information about the particular needs at ImagePhone.

However, if you don't know what the limiting factor is, you might ask about the kinds of problems that increases in sales, R&D, or new products might produce. In this case, you are probably anticipating problems, and you might need to explore several diagrams that reflect a variety of mental models about what could happen in the future. In each one, a different variable from the growth loop might be the driver of the limiting loop.

In causal loop diagrams, the limit is often shown as a separate variable linked by an arrow to a constraining action—it's the same diagram as a balancing loop with a goal. The limit may be physical—for example, customer service capacity—or it may be a mental or emotional limit, such as management's capacity to share power.

The link between the limiting loop and the growth loop may take two forms. Sometimes the limiting loop comes around to affect the variable that triggered it. In ImagePhone's case, inability to provide customer service comes back to affect sales, which originally triggered the need for service. This direction of feedback throughout the structure sometimes traces a horizontal "figure-8."

In other cases, the driving variable in the reinforcing loop may be different than the variable that is directly affected by the balancing loop. In the case of the hotel, for example, the triggering variable is management's emphasis on empowerment, which affects a series of variables and comes back to impact responsiveness to guests, elsewhere in the reinforcing loop. This example illustrates that while the "Limits to Success" archetype reflects the general structural pattern of a reinforcing loop interlocking with a balancing loop, it does not always match any one specific pattern (like the figure-8 structure).

A Deeper Look at the "Limits to Success" Structure

Various analogies have been used to describe the "Limits to Success" archetype. One way of looking at it is as a structure in which the accelerator is attached to the brakes. Another way of seeing it is as a gardener who sows the "seeds of destruction" while tending to the growth of the plants. A third way of looking at this archetype is to see it as similar to stuffing an empty trash bag, where filling it is easy in the beginning but gets harder and harder as the bag reaches its limits. Each of these analogies reveals useful insights about this archetype.

Doing the Two-Step

All three of the above analogies recognize the tell-tale, two-step nature of "Limits to Success." The first step is the reinforcing process, which produces the growth phase. The belief or hope of the participants in the system is that, once the growth mechanism begins to operate, it will continue. If they recognize the reinforcing nature of the process, they may even realize that the growth will accelerate. They might actively promote acceleration by applying more of whatever encourages the growth: new products, more people, and so forth.

The second step is the mounting—but delayed—impact of the limiting factor: the brakes, or the "seeds of destruction." It is important to recognize the impact of both the delay and the limit. One reason the second step often goes unnoticed for a while is that it doesn't take effect until time has gone by. This is because the initial capacity of the system is usually able to handle the early stages of growth. By the time the existing capacity has been outstripped by continued growth, however, participants in the system may be lulled into thinking that the engine of growth is unstoppable. This belief prevents them from looking for potential limits. For example, a series of successful new product introductions sweeps the company off its feet, or a pile of thank-you letters from satisfied guests and a steady stream of hotel-room reservations validate the empowerment campaign.

This second step has another common aspect: It often is connected with some part of the enterprise that is remote from the engine of growth. It may be outside the experience of the people running the growing mechanism; it may be in a more mundane, less interesting part of the enterprise. For example, at ImagePhone general management and organizational structure were not part of Miriam's and Joe's expertise, and customer service and human resources—the key limits in their company's system—didn't interest them.

Sometimes the limit is related to a so-called "undiscussable." At the hotels, no one would have brought up the question of whether the empowerment campaign meant that staff might ultimately be given authority to manage the place. Management assumed that only *they* would manage. Likewise, the desire to be positive and supportive about creating a sense of community inhibited people from bringing up potential negative or difficult consequences.

Stepping on the Brake

Note again that the second loop in the "Limits to Success" archetype is a balancing process. The dynamic of a balancing loop is to bring the system back into "balance" relative to either a goal (explicit or implicit) or a system limit (real or perceived). Whenever a system begins to deviate from its goal or capacity, a balancing process is activated that tries to close the gap between the actual state and the goal or between actual capacity and demand for capacity. The faster or more vigorous the growth, the more rapidly the gap grows, and hence the stronger the balancing force that tries to close the gap.

The implication of this dynamic is that the instinctive reaction to the slowdown of growth—"step harder on the accelerator"—actually produces the opposite of the intended effect—unknowingly activating the brake as well. Worse, the braking effect often is *not* a deliberate management action; it happens because of the structure of the system. This overall paradoxical dynamic is what contains the "seeds of destruction" for the system.

Remember, the engine of growth is a reinforcing process, which tends to accelerate in whatever direction it is set to moving. Initially, it is set spinning in a positive growth direction; for a while, the more it is pushed, the more it grows. However, when the balancing process is activated (which often goes unnoticed for some time), it may come around and eventually reverse the direction of the reinforcing process. This happens when the slowing effects of the balancing loop overpower the growing efforts of the reinforcing loop (a classic case of a shift in loop dominance).

However, if the limiting process goes unnoticed for even a little while and increasing energy is put into the engine of growth, that reinforcing loop can go into a "death spiral," leading to a rapid decline in the organization's fortunes. Each push on the accelerator, intended to push past the limit and return to growth, actually strengthens the impact of the limit until it overpowers all efforts at pumping up the engine of growth. When ImagePhone ignored its management and structural issues and just pushed for improved sales, they actually hastened their demise. If the hotels increased their cheerleading for empowerment without addressing the constraints, staff frustration might lead to actual sabotage instead of improved guest loyalty.

MANAGING "LIMITS TO SUCCESS"

At this point you might be asking yourself, "Does all growth *have* to hit a limit?" When we look around at the natural world and scan the pages of history, the answer seems to be yes—nothing grows forever. Therefore, we believe that you can't ignore the "Limits to Success" structure, but you *can* anticipate and manage it. The highest leverage in managing a "Limits to Success" situation lies in acting early to address a limit *before* it starts undermining your efforts. Here are some guidelines:

- **Use the archetype *before* you hit a limit.**

This archetype is most helpful when used before you hit a limit. That way, you can see how the cumulative effects of continued success might lead to future problems. "Limits to Success" can highlight potential problems by raising questions such as, "What kinds of pressures are building or could build in the organization as a result of growth?" By tracing the implications of these pressures through a causal loop diagram of the system, identifying the limits, and working to remove them before the limit is reached, you can release the pressure before an organizational gasket blows.

- **Assume that you will hit various limits, and try to clarify which ones they might be.**

As you make plans for growth, automatically assume that *something* will eventually limit the growth, and then go looking for those limits. Study other companies or groups who have embarked on similar ventures to see what limits they may have encountered on their journey of growth. Walk yourself through your processes or services, looking at them from the point of view of all members of the organization as well as that of the customers, suppliers, and other outsiders. Ask again how growth could be limited by factors in a number of other areas: customer service, training, delivery. And don't overlook intangible elements—attitudes, values, beliefs, feelings, and relationships.

- **Avoid the temptation to push the system harder once you reach a limit.**

Once limits kick in and you encounter the balancing forces that are working against your engine of growth, avoid the knee-jerk reaction of just applying more of what initially worked. Remember, the harder we push, the harder the system pushes back—and, the faster it may unravel. The real leverage in a "Limits to Success" situation does not lie in pushing harder on the engine of growth, but in finding and managing the factor or factors that are limiting success while there is still time and money to do so. This strategy may involve taking politically difficult steps, such as investing in new capacity before it is actually needed or developing new management systems when all your instincts are screaming that more R&D is needed instead.

 ## In Summary

The "Limits to Success" story is very different from the two preceding archetypes, "Fixes That Fail" and "Shifting the Burden." However, taken together, these three are the most easily recognizable systemic structures for most people. "Limits to Success" is particularly valuable as a touchstone in modern culture. Western society places such a strong emphasis on growth for growth's sake—the "bigger is better" syndrome. This archetype is an important and necessary reminder that there *are* limits, but that we can learn what they are, how they may emerge, and how to work with them.

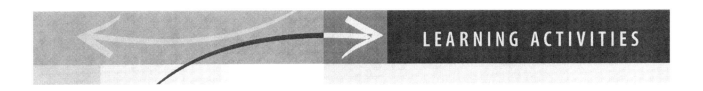

Now that you've learned about "Limits to Success," try your hand at the Learning Activities below. These exercises will give you an opportunity to identify "Limits to Success" dynamics in case studies, and to analyze a "Limits to Success" story from your own experience.

In each Learning Activity, you will be asked to provide:

- A statement of the theme of the story
- A list of key variables
- A graph of the key variables' distinctive behavior over time
- A causal loop diagram of the systemic structure generating the "Limits to Success" situation.

After completing the Learning Activities below, compare your responses with those in Appendix A. Don't worry if your responses look different from the ones in the appendix; there's no one right "answer" in a systems thinking analysis. These activities are mainly meant to get you thinking about the themes, patterns of behavior, and systemic structure of the archetypes.

ACTIVITY 1   LIMITS TO QUALITY

The Story ➤ National Courier, a package expediting company, implements a quality initiative. After the management speeches, training sessions, and team meetings, both line workers and managers begin to initiate some quality improvement projects and then an increase in the actual quality of services, especially tracking and on-time pick-ups. These improvements highlight the importance of the quality initiative and generate motivation to do even more. The company sets up additional quality improvement projects.

As people get involved with the projects, they realize they need more skills related to the issues they're surfacing; for example, financial accounting concepts and operations management. The training department goes into overdrive to find, create, and deliver training, but their staff and their budget are too limited to meet the growing need for training. As a result, staff keeps falling behind in their skills.

Eventually, people become discouraged by their inability to implement or pursue the improvements they want to make. The number of quality improvement projects tapers off, and enthusiasm for the whole idea just fizzles away.

INSTRUCTIONS

1. Summarize the "Limits to Success" theme in this story in two or three sentences.

2. Identify the key variables in the story.

   The growth engine is when _____ begin. As a result, _____

   increases, so _____ goes up. _____ then increases, which

   reinforces the increase in the original factor. After a while, the _____

   begins to grow, but it is constrained by _____, which reduces the

   _____. As a result, people do not develop the _____ the

   projects, which undermines further growth in improvement projects.

3. Graph the behavior over time of National Courier's quality initiatives.

4. Using the blank systems archetype template below, fill in the diagram with the variables. You may add extra variables in any loop. Label all your arrows with an "s" or an "o" to show "same" or "opposite" change.

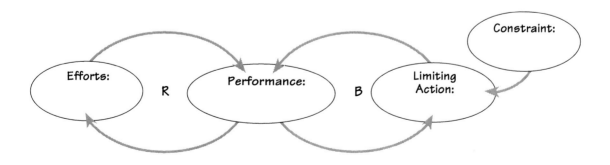

ACTIVITY 2   **CAN RISING SALES HURT IN THE LONG RUN?**

The Story ➤ OCP, a laser printer manufacturer, is discussing its current growth strategy. During a key meeting, the director of operations suggests that the strategy task force examine a proposal from the sales and marketing department for a new marketing campaign. Upper management is confident that the continued focus on marketing will produce good results. For their products, marketing has always had a strong effect on sales, so it makes sense to run some new marketing campaigns. Some of the increased revenues will then be invested in continuing the marketing initiatives and trying new programs.

The sales & marketing VP almost gloats over the prospect of an increasing customer base. Like other companies in the office-equipment industry, OCP knows that there's substantial revenue not only in selling more of its high-end products but also in providing peripherals such as (in OCP's case) toner cartridges, cleaning kits, and service contracts. But during the strategy task force meeting, the tech-support manager chimes in with a provocative question: What will happen to demand for technical assistance when there are a lot more of the high-end printers with advanced features out in homes and offices around the country? "Won't we be swamped with calls?" she asks. "The fastest way to turn people off is not being able to help them out. They'll just go to their local generic laser printer service shop and forget about us. Then next time, they'll buy their printer from someone else."

INSTRUCTIONS

1. Summarize the generic "Limits to Success" theme in this story in two or three sentences.

2. Identify the key variables in the story:

Engine of growth:

Constraint on growth:

Limiting process:

Limiting factor:

3. Graph the possible behavior over time of OCP's future sales.

4. Using the blank systems archetype template below, fill in the diagram with the variables you identified. You may have additional variables or loops. Label each of your arrows with an "s" or an "o," and then label each loop in your diagram with an "R" or a "B" to indicate "reinforcing" and "balancing" processes.

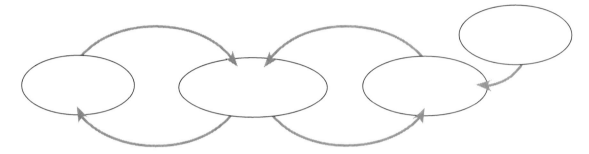

ACTIVITY 3   AN INTERNET PROVIDER GETS A BUSY SIGNAL[1]

The Story ➤ In the highly competitive universe of Internet service providers, increasing market share is essential both to survival and to growth because it increases economies of scale as well as overall attractiveness. SurfBoard, a new and rapidly expanding provider, starts its business by charging subscribers a monthly fee plus an hourly usage fee. This pricing structure encourages cost-conscious users to handle email off-line and limit the time they spend "surfing" the 'Net. To justify higher rates, SurfBoard offers value-added services.

One day, however, SurfBoard decides to launch a flat-fee plan on top of an aggressive marketing campaign. The objective of both these efforts is to increase the company's customer base. Within weeks, SurfBoard has added more than a million new subscribers.

However, this success is quickly followed by increasing complaints about the difficulty of actually logging on. Although the company had expected to attract new users, it is completely unprepared for the actual volume of demand. There's nowhere near enough modems to handle the volume of calls, and no mechanism for limiting the on-line time of users who sign on early in the day just to hold open their access. Regular users are blocked from doing research, sending and receiving email, and transmitting electronic files.

In response to these difficulties, some customers file lawsuits and others switch to alternative providers. Everyone bad-mouths SurfBoard. Although the company has taken measures to remedy the situation—increasing modem capacity and giving refunds—it could take years for them to restore consumer confidence and regain market growth momentum.

INSTRUCTIONS

1. Summarize the "Limits to Success" theme in this story in two or three sentences.

2. Identify the key variables in the story.

   Engine of growth:

   Constraint on growth:

   Limiting process:

   Limiting factor:

3. Graph the behavior of the variable that SurfBoard wanted to grow.

4. In the space below, draw a causal loop diagram using the variables you identified. Label each arrow with an "s" or an "o," and each loop with an "R" or a "B."

ACTIVITY 4 **YOUR OWN "LIMITS TO SUCCESS"**

INSTRUCTIONS

Follow the steps below.

STEP 1: Choose a problem or situation from work, home, community, or elsewhere that might be a "Limits to Success" situation. Pick one that has some history so you can clearly see actual trends and the impact of actual interventions.

STEP 2: Make some notes about the story, enough to remind yourself of what has been happening.

STEP 3: Summarize the story in a couple of sentences. (You may find it is easier to come back to this step after you have worked with the variables and the loop diagram.)

STEP 4: List the key variables in the story. If your initial list is quite long (more than six or seven variables), try aggregating some of them and possibly narrowing the focus of the story.

Engine of growth:

Constraint on growth:

Limiting process:

Limiting factor:

STEP 5: Draw the pattern of behavior over time of the growing variable(s). To confirm your graph, check with colleagues, friends, or family members to see whether your memory of the pattern of behavior matches theirs. The key to identifying a "Limits to Success" dynamic is the S-shaped curve of performance that grows and then levels off.

STEP 6: Draw a causal loop diagram of your situation. Show all the necessary key variables to either the growth or limiting process loops.

To confirm your diagram, walk through the logic of the loops. Does growth happen as the loop indicates? Does the limiting process come back and slow down or reverse the growth? Did you indicate the delays?

Check the validity of your diagram further by asking whether the limiting process could ultimately reverse growth and lead to the demise of the enterprise.

Finally, validate and broaden your insight by showing your diagram to a friend, colleague, or family member. Remember to position it as your "first-draft" attempt to understand what has been going on. Explain the diagram in terms of the growth process and then the limiting process. Then be sure to ask the person what he or she thinks and whether your explanation makes sense. Don't worry if your versions are different. Everyone's version of the story is a unique mental model, and the point is to learn more about the mental models at work in the problems facing us.

Notes

1. From "How America Online Grew into a Busy Signal," by Don Seville, *The Systems Thinker*, Volume 8, Number 4, May 1997 (Pegasus Communications, Inc.).

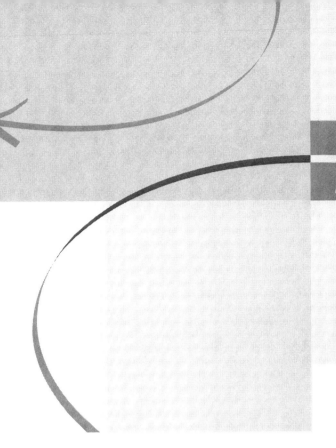

Drifting Goals

In a "Drifting Goals" situation, a gap between desired performance and current reality can be resolved either by taking corrective action to achieve the goal or by lowering the goal. The gap is often resolved by a gradual lowering of the goal. Over time, the performance level also drifts downward. This drift may happen so gradually, even without deliberate action, that the organization is not even aware of its impact.

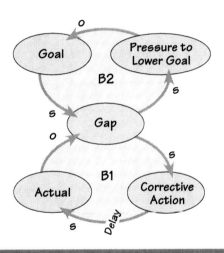

THE STORYLINE:
Trouble with Tato Bits[1]

Western Foods is committed to producing quality Tato Bits with chunky insides and a light, crispy coating. In order to increase efficiency, the company institutes a series of cost-cutting initiatives. Plant managers increase line speeds and change cooking and storage methods.

Over the next five years, sales of Tato Bits begin to slip. Managers assume there has been a change in people's eating habits. Two more years go by, and sales continue to decline. Western Foods decides to conduct consumer research studies. Feedback reveals that the taste and consistency of Tato Bits has changed for the worse.

Further analysis suggests that the gap between the quality standard and actual Tato Bit quality had first appeared more than 10 years ago. The gap should have signaled management that Western's processes, equipment, or ingredients needed attention and possible investment. However, the company was distracted by its cost-control campaign, and the quality standard was allowed to drift in favor of other changes and the need to keep production moving. Very slowly, almost imperceptibly, quality had slid below consumers' level of tolerance.

THE "BOILED FROG" SYNDROME: THE GENERIC STORY BEHIND "DRIFTING GOALS"[2]

The "Drifting Goals" story can be illustrated by the account of the "boiled frog" syndrome. It is an old adage that if you put a frog in a pot of boiling water, it will leap out. But if you put it in a pot of lukewarm water and turn up the heat slowly, the frog will stay in the pot until it boils to death because its sensing mechanism cannot detect gradual changes in temperature. The frog story captures "Drifting Goals" because it describes a scenario in which performance or expectations degrade imperceptively over a long period of time.

A "Drifting Goals" situation starts when there is a gap between desired performance and actual performance. To close the gap, one choice is to take corrective action, which requires time, effort, funds, and/or attention. Taking corrective action, however, can pose several problems. First, there is often no guarantee that it will work. In addition, because its effects are realized only after a delay, there may be little organizational patience for it. Furthermore, taking corrective action may mean acknowledging that something is wrong, which can lead to the assumption that someone should be blamed and punished. This, in turn, may bring about conflict as different parties try to place blame elsewhere—something to be avoided in most organizations.

The other choice is to lower the desired performance, or the goal, toward the level of actual performance. The gap disappears, but so does the pressure to take corrective action to improve the actual state. Lowering one's goals isn't always a bad thing. Sometimes it's wise to adjust initial goals, when they turn out to be misdirected or inappropriate, or when there are extenuating circumstances that require us to be flexible. However, new priorities, other implicit goals of the system, or daily survival pressures may lead us to rationalize that the goal needed correction or that our organization will resume the old standard once "everything settles down." Distinguishing between legitimate adjustments and truly eroding goals is the key challenge in a "Drifting Goals" situation.

"Drifting Goals" doesn't always have to lead to declining levels of performance. This archetype can also be reversed into a case where goals and standards continually improve. In this scenario, every time we meet a standard and close a performance gap, we raise our goal even higher. The gap between desired and actual performance opens once again, and we move into action to bring performance into line with the new goal. This version of "Drifting Goals" underlies quality-improvement and self-development programs. It can sometimes drive work group, academic, and family dynamics in which good performance is recognized in such a way that it stimulates even higher performance levels.

CHANGING PERFORMANCE AND STANDARDS: BEHAVIOR OVER TIME IN "DRIFTING GOALS"

This archetype can show several different patterns of behavior over time (see Figure 5.1, "Behavior Over Time in 'Drifting Goals'"). When this structure is driven by the "lower goal" loop, either the goal declines while actual stays steady because no corrective action is taken (5.1a), or the actual state declines in line with declines in the goal (5.1b). On the other hand, when this structure is driven by the "corrective action" loop, either the goal stays the same and actual improves (5.1c) or both the goal and actual improve in a virtuous reinforcing cycle (5.1d). The two loops may also take turns dominating, in which case the two lines can "meet in the middle," as the goal declines while some corrective action is taken (5.1e and 5.1f).

FIGURE 5.1

Behavior Over Time in "Drifting Goals"

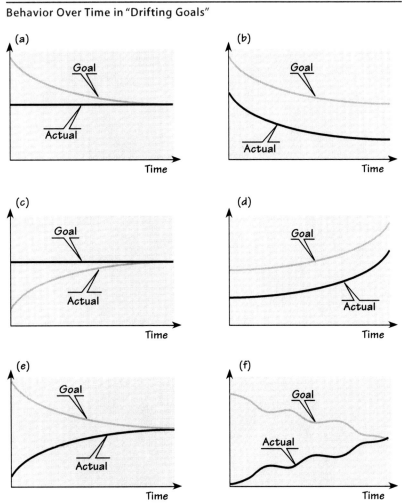

THE SYSTEMIC STRUCTURE BEHIND "DRIFTING GOALS"

At the core of a "Drifting Goals" dynamic are two linked balancing processes (see Figure 5.2, "The Systemic Structure Behind 'Drifting Goals'"). The first balancing loop (B1) consists of the actual performance, a gap between actual and a desired goal, and a corrective action that would close the gap. This loop also contains a delay between corrective action and the impact of that action on actual performance, indicating that it usually takes a relatively longer time to feel the effects of the corrective action.

If there is no difference between the goal and actual performance, the gap is zero. This means that no action is required, neither to improve the situation nor to lower the goal. Of course, this is almost never the case in real life. There is always change and movement in one direction or another. In the "Drifting Goals" structure, one of three possible dynamics can happen:

- The "corrective action" loop can dominate.

- The "lower goal" loop can dominate.

- Dominance can shift back and forth between the two.

Unfortunately, in many real settings, the dynamic of lowering goals has a tendency to dominate the most often.

A healthy response to a gap between a goal and actual would be to take corrective actions to move the actual condition toward one's goals. This means that a gap will initiate actions to correct or improve the actual state, which in time will move the actual up toward the goal (B1). As the gap shrinks or disappears, the pressure to lower goals now becomes a pressure to *increase* goals, which increases the gap again (B2). This triggers another round of corrective actions and traces a figure-8 dynamic of ever-increasing improvements in both the goal and the actual performance (Figure 5.1d).

Unfortunately, the more common scenario is that when there is a gap between desired and actual performance, people in the system often respond by lowering the goal. This doesn't mean that we are deliberately being lazy or intentionally reducing the quality of our work. As in the case of Tato Bits, the organization simply responds to changing pressures in the environment by doing whatever makes sense in the moment. So, without some specific focus on that particular performance variable, it just makes more sense to focus on other pressing needs, and the meaning of high quality becomes something that is "good enough." When this happens, the figure-8 structure is driven in reverse. By lowering the goal and reducing the gap (B2), we send a message that corrective (or improvement) actions are not needed. This often results in a drift in actual performance, as we become even less likely to take corrective actions (B1). The resultant gap triggers another round of goal erosion and further undermining of corrective actions (Figure 5.1b).

FIGURE 5.2

The Systemic Structure Behind "Drifting Goals"

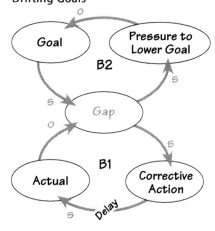

As you can see, either loop can drive this archetype into two very different outcomes. The third possibility is when adjustments are made in *both* loops, leading to a pattern where the goal and actual meet somewhere in the middle (Figure 5.1e). Although the behaviors are shown as smooth curves, they are more likely to oscillate in a trending fashion, as all balancing loops with delay behave (Figure 5.1f).

APPLYING STRUCTURE TO STORY

In the story about Western Foods and Tato Bits, we saw a classic "Drifting Goals" situation in action. Let's look at a causal loop diagram representation of the problem to see what this archetype has to teach us about eroding standards (see Figure 5.3, "Drifting Quality of Tato Bits"). In this situation, when changes in the production process created a gap between Tato Bits quality and the company's quality standard, this should have signaled the need to adjust Western's processes or ingredients to close the gap (B3). However, the drift in quality occurred little by little over a long period of time, so the company did not even perceive the gap. Initially, the customers did not notice the drop in actual quality either; therefore, there was no immediate feedback to the company that their actions had negatively affected the quality. So, instead of increasing investments in the product, Western Foods launched some cost-cutting initiatives that, in essence, lowered their quality standard for Tato Bits even further (B4). This figure-8 dynamic of lowering standards (done indirectly through cost-cutting measures), which led to actions to cut quality (since actual was now higher than the goal), eventually led to a drop in sales as well, as customers stopped buying the inferior Tato Bits.

FIGURE 5.3

Drifting Quality of Tato Bits

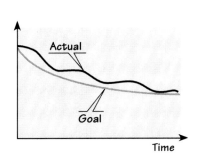

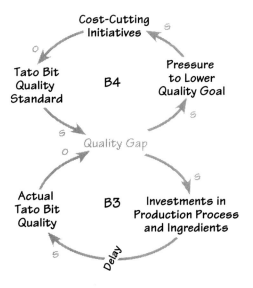

DIAGRAMMING "DRIFTING GOALS"

The process of diagramming a "Drifting Goals" situation usually starts with someone noticing that a particular performance variable is lower than what is desired, and that it has been deteriorating over time. That is, at some point someone (customers, suppliers, line workers, marketing) realizes there is a gap between what is desired and what is really happening. The first step is to identify the corrective actions that are (or should be) currently in operation to close the gap. Next, identify the pressures that the various actors involved with the performance variable feel when a gap opens up, and map those onto the "lower goal" balancing loop of the diagram.

A DEEPER LOOK AT "DRIFTING GOALS"

Eroding performance figures are usually the tip-off that "Drifting Goals" is at work and that real corrective actions necessary to meet the targets are not being taken. The presence of the "Drifting Goals" structure may also indicate that current targets are determined more by past levels of performance than by some absolute standard such as zero defects or by some outside requirement such as customer needs. Finally, the fact that an individual or organization seems to be constantly in crisis, always struggling to meet immediate demands, signals a "Drifting Goals" scenario at work. Under these conditions, it's especially easy to lose sight of the original vision, a higher standard, or the long-term view.

The "Drifting Goals" structure resembles "Shifting the Burden" in several respects. In "Drifting Goals," lowering standards closes the gap between a goal and actual performance much faster than corrective action does, and often takes much less time, effort, and investment. This is a kind of quick fix, whereas the corrective-action balancing loop in "Drifting Goals" constitutes a more fundamental solution. The burden for solving the problem (the gap between desired and actual reality) is shifted to an easy option—lowering the goal—rather than the more difficult or costly option of improving actual performance. In "Shifting the Burden," actions taken to change a goal draw attention and energy away from the fundamental solution and reflect deliberate, short-term decisions. In effect, the unintended side-effect in "Shifting the Burden" actually *undermines* our ability to take action to improve matters. In "Drifting Goals," the erosion of goals happens more insidiously, without any deliberate action.

MANAGING "DRIFTING GOALS"

Getting a grip on "Drifting Goals" or avoiding this dynamic altogether can be quite challenging. Here are some guidelines:

- **Identify what's drifting.**

Specify the goal, standard, or performance measure that could drift or that has deteriorated or oscillated over time. Ask yourself, What exactly has been drifting?

- **Check for competing goals.**

Consider whether the system contains other goals that are explicitly or implicitly in conflict with the first goal. If possible, determine how to reconcile this conflict.

- **Identify what's driving the setting of goals.**

With all the goals you identified in mind, determine what drives the setting of goals. Is it competitors, customers, or internal policy? Goals located outside the system are less susceptible to pressures to drift.

- **Explore procedures for correcting gaps.**

Identify the standard operating procedures for correcting gaps, and make sure they do not contribute to slippage in standards. Also find out whether goal setting is linked most strongly to past performance: That's fine when performance is improving, but disastrous when it slips.

- **Reestablish the organization's vision.**

Clarify the organization's original vision, and consider ways to motivate everyone to maintain the goals needed to achieve the vision.

 ## In Summary

"Drifting Goals" ties into several other archetypal structures. At its simplest, it is the story of a "good balancing loop (the 'corrective action' one) gone astray." The "lower goal" balancing loop in the "Drifting Goals" structure represents a common tendency to let goals slide rather than do the necessary work to meet them. As we saw earlier, "Drifting Goals" is also a variation on the "Shifting the Burden" theme: Instead of committing to doing one's best, the individual or the organization opts for the quick fix, the ready relief. Finally, "Drifting Goals" can explain how an organization gets into the "Growth and Underinvestment" trap, as we'll see in the next section. When growth puts pressure on aspects of performance that are hard to manage, estimate, or predict, the intention to maintain growth slides, and the investment that might have supported the growth is minimized, withheld, or even withdrawn.

Now that you've learned about "Drifting Goals," try your hand at the Learning Activities below. These exercises will give you an opportunity to identify "Drifting Goals" dynamics in stories, and to analyze a "Drifting Goals" story from your own experience.

In each Learning Activity, you will be asked to provide:

• A statement of the theme of the story

• A list of key variables

• A graph of the key variables' distinctive behavior over time

• A causal loop diagram of the systemic structure generating the "Drifting Goals" situation.

After completing the Learning Activities below, compare your responses with those in Appendix A. Don't worry if your responses look different from the ones in the appendix; there's no one right "answer" in a systems thinking analysis. These activities are mainly meant to get you thinking about the themes, patterns of behavior, and systemic structure of the archetypes.

Activity 1   **THE CASE OF THE DRIFTING PRODUCTION BUDGET**

The Story ➤ Nature Unlimited, a company that produces a nature-film series, has decided to take a new approach to a big new project. Maria, the producer; Franco, the production department manager; and Roxanne, the facility director, have just concluded a long project-planning meeting with a clearly laid out budget and schedule. A new series of checkpoints on the schedule, they hope, will keep them on track with time and expenses, and two additional project-review sessions will keep the corporate office in the loop with funding approvals.

Maria gets to work on the project. She tells Franco that she'd like to bring in top scripting talent, because a good script almost guarantees an easy production. "Go ahead, Maria," Franco agrees. "You know the business." Happily for Maria, Corporate loves the script and reemphasizes the importance of the video having the right "look" to attract buyers. Maria and Franco track down Roxanne in the hallway. "Roxanne," they say, "if Corporate likes this one, you know they'll come back to us to fund the rest of the series. Gotta pour on what it takes."

Preproduction pressures put Maria into overdrive searching for perfect scenic locations and just the right narration talent. "Franco," she gushes, "it's just what Corporate's looking for. They're gonna eat up this video." She's right: Corporate adores the location stills and the casting tapes.

Of course, getting the production equipment, the facilities for the narrators and crew, and meals to the shoot locations proves pretty expensive, but "it's what Corporate wants," Maria and Franco decide. Corporate goes crazy for the rough-cut takes and chooses some very slick effects for opening titles and transitions. "See?" Maria crows. "We knew they wanted top-drawer work."

At the end of the six weeks, Roxanne calls Maria and Franco into her office. Pointing to a pile of invoices and a print-out from the purchasing department, Roxanne demands, "What happened to our goal of staying within the budget? We're gonna go broke on this one film!"

INSTRUCTIONS

1. Summarize the "Drifting Goals" theme in this story in two or three sentences.

2. Identify the key variables in the story. (Variables in brackets do not necessarily need to appear in your final causal loop diagram.)

The explicit goal was to _____.

At several points in the production process, Maria and Franco could have noticed a

_____ between the goal and _____.

Ideally, they would have _____ to stay in line with the goal.

However, they were motivated by pressure to _____ and

_____ the original goal.

[As a result, _____ got higher and higher while Corporate was

increasingly _____.]

3. Graph what happens over time to the original goal and to the activity it was supposed to control.

4. Fill in the blank systems archetype template below with the key variables from the story. Label each arrow with an "s" or an "o," and add any important delays.

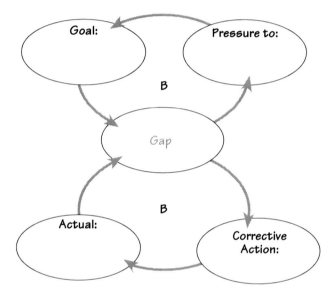

5. How might Nature Unlimited turn its troubling situation around?

ACTIVITY 2   YOUR OWN "DRIFTING GOALS" STORY

INSTRUCTIONS

Follow the steps below.

STEP 1: Choose a possible "Drifting Goals" situation from work, home, community, or else-where. Pick a situation that has some history so you can clearly see actual trends.

STEP 2: Make some notes about the story, enough to remind yourself of what has been happening.

STEP 3: Summarize the story in a couple of sentences. (You may find it is easier to come back to this step after you have worked with the variables and the loop diagram.)

STEP 4: List the key variables in the situation.

The goal:

The intended corrective action:

Actual performance:

Source of pressure to change the goal:

STEP 5: Draw the behavior over time of the goal and the actual performance.
To confirm your graph, check with colleagues, friends, or family members to see whether your memory of the pattern of behavior matches theirs.

STEP 6: Using the "Drifting Goals" causal loop template, diagram your situation, labeling all arrows and loops.

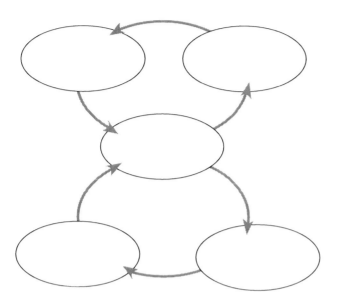

To confirm your diagram, walk through the logic of the loops. Does the diagram show two balancing processes? What was the original goal and the corrective action? How is actual performance linked with perception of the gap and then pressure to change the original goal? If there is an implicit goal that contributes to the pressure to change, show it as a variable outside the top loop, linked to "Pressure to Lower Goal."

Validate and broaden your insights by showing your diagram to a friend, colleague, or family member. Remember to position it as your "first-draft" attempt to understand what has been going on. Explain your diagram in terms of how an original goal or performance standard changed over time and the pressures that might have led to that change. Be sure to ask what the other person thinks and whether this explanation makes sense. Don't worry if your versions are different. Everyone's version is a unique mental model, and the point is to learn which mental models are at work in the problems facing us.

STEP 7: Is there any way of anchoring the goal in your story, so that it no longer drifts? Explain.

Notes

1. From "Using 'Drifting Goals' to Keep Your Eye on the Vision," *Systems Archetypes II: Using Systems Archetypes to Take Effective Action,* by Daniel H. Kim (Pegasus Communications, Inc., 1994).

2. Adapted from "'Drifting Goals': The 'Boiled Frog' Syndrome," *Systems Archetypes I: Diagnosing Systemic Issues and Designing High-Leverage Interventions,* by Daniel H. Kim (Pegasus Communications, Inc., 1992).

SECTION 6

Growth and Underinvestment

In a "Growth and Underinvestment" situation, growth approaches a limit that could be eliminated or postponed if capacity investments were made. Instead, as a result of policies or delays in the system, demand (or performance) degrades, limiting further growth. The declining demand then leads to further withholding of investment or even reductions in capacity, causing even worse performance.

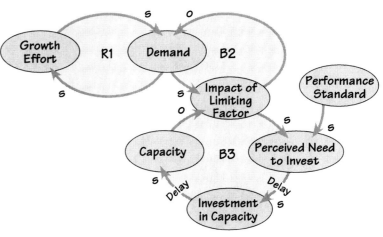

THE STORYLINE:

Backlog at Electric House[1]

Mark Preminger, the CEO of Electric House, a capital equipment manufacturer, lived through an industry downturn in which Electric House was saddled with too much capacity. He is cautious about expanding. However, the company's product is selling well, and a backlog has begun piling up—three months' worth of orders at first, then four, then five. Preminger continues to believe that the rise in customer orders is just a temporary spurt. When the backlog grows to six months, however, he finally agrees to expand production capacity.

It takes about a year-and-a-half for the additional capacity to come online. In the meantime, demand trails off as people find alternative sources. Electric House gradually works off the backlog and then lives through a disappointing period in which sales perk up a bit, but not at the levels forecasted during the expansion decision. Finally, orders start to pick up again. After a couple of years, the company experiences a similar backlog, and Preminger is even more reluctant to invest in new capacity because of what he sees as a continual, unpredictable cycle of growing and falling demand.

"PLAYING WITH A WOODEN RACKET": THE GENERIC STORY BEHIND "GROWTH AND UNDERINVESTMENT"

Do you recall the first time you picked up a tennis racket? Perhaps it was an old wooden racket you found in your garage, or one that a friend had outgrown. You weren't really sure you had what it took to play—you did not even know whether you'd like the sport. But you tried playing a few games a week with the beat-up racket, picking up some basic moves and even sustaining a few volleys. After a month or so, though, you couldn't seem to improve beyond a certain level. If you were a *little* better, you might have willingly invested in a new, high-performance racket. But you decided that tennis just isn't for you.

This scenario is an example of the "Growth and Underinvestment" archetype at work. In this archetype, an individual or organization experiences a growth in opportunity or demand that begins to outstrip capacity. Persistent capacity shortfalls lead to reduced performance. Demand or motivation for maintaining high performance then drops. This fall in demand or motivation is seen as a reason for not making future investments in capacity rather than as a *symptom* of continued underinvestment and falling demand. In the end, shutting down production or looking for different opportunities may seem to be the only appropriate action.

MULTIPLE TREND LINES: "GROWTH AND UNDERINVESTMENT" OVER TIME

A graph of the distinctive behavior over time of "Growth and Underinvestment" includes at least four variables: demand, capacity, perceived need to invest, and capacity investments (see Figure 6.1, "Behavior Over Time in 'Growth and Underinvestment'"). The dynamics of this structure are more precisely related than most of the other archetypes. In particular, the perceived need to invest drives the actual investments, which in turn affects capacity, which then affects demand. The gap between demand and capacity then affects perceived need to invest, thus closing the loop. The growth effort (not shown) may behave in various ways, depending on the organizational circumstances. It may, for example, be pegged at a steady level by policy regardless of where demand or capacity is, or it may be increased whenever demand is not growing.

In Figure 6.1, we can see some noteworthy points in the interrelated behavior among the four variables. Time "A" is when demand begins to exceed capacity, which causes the perceived need to invest to rise. After some delay (depending on the organization), capacity investments are

FIGURE 6.1

Behavior Over Time in "Growth and Underinvestment"

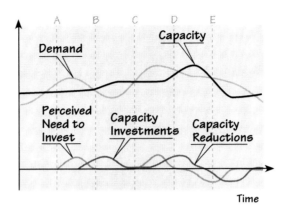

made and capacity starts to increase. When capacity begins exceeding demand at time "B" (because of falling demand due to shortage and a rise in capacity due to investments), perceived need to invest drops to zero. Because of delays, capacity continues to grow as investments in the pipeline come online, so capacity continues to rise above demand. With excess capacity, the company is better able to serve its customers, so demand increases again until it begins exceeding capacity again at time "C"—and the cycle repeats.

However, there is danger lurking in these ups and downs. In today's competitive environment, a company is not likely to be able to keep drawing customers back each time they expand capacity to meet customers' needs. The rises and peaks of demand can become smaller and smaller each time, as customers defect to other suppliers. The company can then find itself in the reverse situation of a downward spiral of adjustments. When the demand doesn't recover after time "D," the company cuts capacity below the demand level (time "E"), so demand falls even lower, which triggers another round of capacity cuts.

 ## A SPECIAL CASE OF "LIMITS TO SUCCESS": THE SYSTEMIC STRUCTURE BEHIND "GROWTH AND UNDERINVESTMENT"

The causal loop diagram template for "Growth and Underinvestment" builds on the "Limits to Success" structure (see Figure 6.2, "The Structure Behind 'Growth and Underinvestment,'" p. 76). The reinforcing loop (R1) is the growth engine, which includes the growth effort and the demand (the variable the organization wants to grow). The growth in loop R1 creates pressures as it strains current limits and as growth is slowed by the impact of the limiting factor(s) represented in loop B2. What makes this a "Growth and Underinvestment" structure is the additional balancing loop (B3) that manages the limiting factor, adjusting it to meet a goal or performance standard that people feel is important. The interplay among these three loops can create a wide range of behaviors.

FIGURE 6.2

The Structure Behind "Growth and Underinvestment"

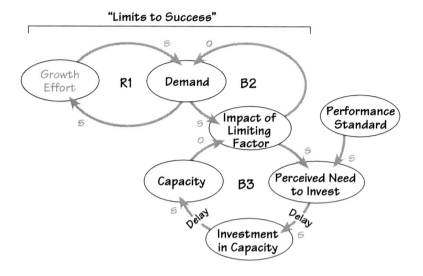

When the impact of the limiting factor differs from the organization's performance standard, the gap increases the perception that capacity investments are needed to overcome the limiting factor (B3). Time begins to play a crucial role here, because there are usually significant delays for perceptions to change and for translating those perceptions into actual investment decisions. Once decisions are made, there is a further delay as it takes time for new capacity to come online. As capacity finally expands, the constraining impact of the limiting factor is reduced, which reverses the direction of B2 and reinvigorates the growth engine. We can see how this works by tracing the feedback that flows through this part of the structure: The eventual increase in capacity reduces or postpones the impact of the limiting factor, which in turn stimulates demand (B2). A rise in demand encourages an increase in the growth effort, which raises demand even more (R1). But the increase in demand once again triggers the impact of the limiting factor, thereby reviving the perceived need to invest (B3).

In this scenario, the critical factor is the difference in how fast each of the balancing loops operates. If B2 functions significantly faster than B3, then the investment that B3 generates may not come into play soon enough to provide needed capacity. On the other hand, if B3 can be activated quickly, it can reverse the situation, as we saw above. In this case, the impact of the limit is removed before its effects can be felt, and the growth engine (R1) continues to chug away happily.

As we explained earlier, this archetype can show a range of possible behaviors. At the extreme end of the range, companies can actually destroy themselves by slashing capacity investment or not investing early enough. This dynamic has been exemplified by several high-tech companies that sold off divisions and laid off employees until the organization could no longer function. Here's how this scenario plays out: When the impact of the limiting factor decreases, there is pressure to *lower the performance standard* rather than invest in capacity. The two balancing loops then begin to function as a single reinforcing loop that has an insidious effect: It responds to a steady decline in growth by continuing to withhold or withdraw investment. This dynamic can choke the growth engine completely and ultimately prove fatal for the enterprise (as shown in the latter part of the behavior over time graph in Figure 6.1).

APPLYING STRUCTURE TO STORY

How would the "Backlog at Electric House" story look mapped onto the "Growth and Underinvestment" template (see Figure 6.3, "'Growth and Underinvestment' at Electric House")? In the past, Electric House had exerted efforts to grow the business; as a result, demand for the company's products had risen (R4), encouraging even more growth efforts. But this very growth triggered an increase in order backlog. As demand—and backlog—increased, the company's production capacity became less and less able to satisfy the demand. Backlog started to accumulate even further, customers grew frustrated, and sales began dropping (B5).

The company realized it needed to invest in production capacity (B6). But there was a delay between the perception of this need and the actual investment decision, and between the decision and the eventual increase in capacity. Therefore, by the time the increased capacity kicked in, demand for Electric House's products had already trailed off as customers went elsewhere. However, the increased capacity eventually reduced backlog, so after a while, customers were attracted again to Electric House, and the cycle of increasing and decreasing demand and backlog began all over again.

FIGURE 6.3

"Growth and Underinvestment" at Electric House

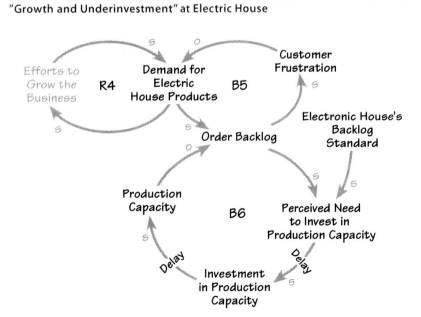

DIAGRAMMING "GROWTH AND UNDERINVESTMENT"

When you prepare to diagram a "Growth and Underinvestment" situation, your attention is likely to be drawn first to oscillating or dropping sales. Determine whether the "Limits to Growth" part of the structure best explains the dynamic. As you map that part of the system, you may encounter issues around how capacity investment decisions are made, which leads to the second balancing loop.

 ## A DEEPER LOOK AT "GROWTH AND UNDERINVESTMENT"

To determine whether a "Growth and Underinvestment" structure is at work, look especially for oscillating trends in demand (whether it's for products, time, resources, capital) and capacity investments to meet that demand. If your organization states that it is pursuing a growth strategy, consider whether the company is planning for enough investment to sustain the eventual growth. When discussion comes up about cost-cutting, layoffs, or reduced investment in response to a change in the market or a drop in demand, explore the possible impacts of these policies on growth. Ask, "How would our decisions affect demand for our products or services? How might we be *creating* new limits by cutting back on capacity investments?"

In addition, as we saw above, the two balancing loops in this archetype can be especially challenging to untangle. We can see that as the growth encounters a limit, a healthy system would operate to anticipate that limit and reduce its impact by adding capacity. However, many companies fail to perceive—and therefore manage—the limit in time. Worse, as the limit begins to slow growth, the business may respond by cutting investment even further, which pushes the overall business downward. Although the organization's members may think that "external forces" are driving demand away, it may be a direct result of their own investment decisions.

 ## MANAGING "GROWTH AND UNDERINVESTMENT"

To avoid falling into the underinvestment trap, you need to develop the ability to anticipate and choose limits rather than letting the system do it for you. This requires having the ability to find ways to remove limits by investing in needed capacity in a timely manner. Accomplishing this is made particularly difficult because this structure contains two sources of significant delay, either of which can derail your efforts. The following sections provide some tips in dealing with these two sources of delay.

Perception Delay

The first delay involves perception—the time it takes to perceive that current performance is deficient enough to take serious action, and the time required to actually begin investing in capacity. Here are some guidelines for managing this especially frustrating delay:

- **Take time early in the growth phase to identify potential limits to growth, especially capacity limits.**

Ask yourself, "If we succeed in growing our sales, what will happen? How much production, customer service, or delivery capacity will we need to respond to potentially higher sales? What will be the impact if we have lower sales?" Studying the market response and the characteristics of target customers during an upswing can help you anticipate these future capacity needs.

- **Make sure that internal systems are set up to respond to growth.**

If you have an aggressive growth strategy and a sluggish internal system for responding to performance shortfalls, you may have created a structural inability to handle continued growth. For example, how much lead time does your manufacturing team need to beef up production? If your salespeople increase sales by 40 percent in a quarter and your plant can expand production at the rate of only 20 percent per quarter, you can expect a backlog to build up quickly.

- **Explore the assumptions driving capacity investment decisions.**

Past performance may be a consideration but should not dominate decisions. Instead, identify the market factors that drive growth. Otherwise, you may make investment decisions that are too dependent on past experience and not sufficiently linked to present or future desires and needs.

- **Ensure that everyone involved has a well-informed set of assumptions (mental models) about the size of the total potential market.**

These assumptions will influence investment decisions.

Capacity-Acquisition Delay

Once a decision is made to invest, a second delay—in capacity acquisition—means that additional time is required for the decision to translate into tangible increases in capacity. In many cases, things may even get worse before they get better. Underestimating this delay can lead you to take premature countermeasures that may only aggravate the situation. For example, you might end up with more capacity than necessary because you overorder while waiting for capacity to come online.

The Market

Managing this archetype also requires the ability to discern the true state of the market. For example, is demand declining because of market changes? Or is *your* demand declining because your actions are limiting your market potential? When you review your organization's performance, how can you tell whether downturns are of your own making or are truly stemming from changes in the market?

Traditional accounting measures and business performance indicators are based on the assumptions that the market is "out there" and that the organization responds as best it can to external events. To see how our actions affect that external environment, we need to identify the feedback loops that connect our actions and the market's behavior. This process requires a deep understanding of what customers really need and how well equipped we are to respond to that need. We must make a link between customer demand and our organization's internal standard of performance. This link sends an early warning signal to invest, shortening the perception delay described above. We can short-circuit the underinvestment loop as well, but to do so we must make investments *before* we receive the traditional signals that usually trigger such decisions. The challenge lies in understanding the market well enough to know the factors that affect demand (for example, delivery, service, quality, price), potential limits, competitors' behavior, and the key investment decisions that affect these limits (capacity, training, R&D, manufacturing processes, and so forth).

 ## In Summary

"Growth and Underinvestment" is a relatively complex, composite archetype. It tells a story that plays out over time and one in which *time delays* themselves are a significant component. This archetype contains a number of dynamics, including an engine of growth, a constraint, and a balancing process with a goal. In essence, we can see it as a coupling of the "Limits to Success" structure with the "Drifting Goals" structure.

"Growth and Underinvestment" is relevant for many areas of an organization—from sales and marketing to production—because it graphically shows the interrelationships between their individual growth efforts and investment decisions. It is therefore especially valuable for demonstrating the unfavorable consequences that can come from fractured, "stovepipe" thinking.

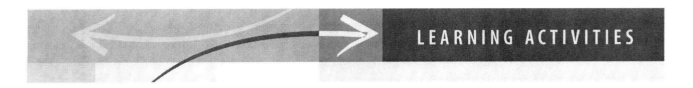

Now that you've learned about "Growth and Underinvestment," try your hand at the Learning Activities below. These exercises will give you an opportunity to identify a "Growth and Underinvestment" dynamic in a story, and to analyze a "Growth and Underinvestment" story from your own experience.

In each Learning Activity, you will be asked to provide:

• A statement of the theme of the story

• A list of key variables

• A graph of the key variables' distinctive behavior over time

• A causal loop diagram of the systemic structure generating the "Growth and Underinvestment" situation.

After completing the Learning Activities below, compare your responses with those in Appendix A. Don't worry if your responses look different from the ones in the appendix; there's no one right "answer" in a systems thinking analysis. These activities are mainly meant to get you thinking about the themes, patterns of behavior, and systemic structure of the archetypes.

ACTIVITY 1   **THE LOW-COST GROWTH DILEMMA[2]**

The Story ➤ ExpressTech has taken the lead in the U.S. mail-order PC business by combining low production costs with a customer base of small businesses and technically knowledgeable users. Low taxes and cheap labor at its midwest headquarters, plus a "no frills" corporate style, have allowed ExpressTech to keep its production costs low relative to competitors'. Consequently, the company can offer its customers a low-cost, high-quality product with dependable customer service. With all these advantages in place, ExpressTech has experienced phenomenal growth.

One day, ExpressTech reaches a critical point at which it has to keep its revenues growing strongly while maintaining quality and service and not losing control of costs. For the first time, the company experiences a drop in sales. The CEO attributes the decline to a backlog of orders from the previous year that have inflated first-quarter results. Continuing sales drops indicate a larger problem—declining customer-service quality.

But finding and training technical and assembly-line workers in the company's rural setting quickly enough to keep up with customer demand is difficult and time consuming. Staff shortages increase customer complaints about delayed deliveries and lead to long waits on customer service lines. By adding 75 new phone lines and expanding its cadre of technical support personnel, ExpressTech manages to cut the time that customers have to wait. Still, some people continue to complain about being left on hold for too long.

INSTRUCTIONS

1. Summarize the "Growth and Underinvestment" theme in this story in two or three sentences.

2. Identify the key variables in the story.

   _____ (the growth variable) was growing, bringing in more and more

   _____, which financed continued growth. As growth continued, the need

   for more _____ (the limiting factor variable) arose. Based on

   a _____ (the standard), ExpressTech perceived a

   growing _____. Although the company responded by increasing

   _____ (the capacity investment variable), there was a

   _____ before the effect of the action could be observed.

3. Graph what happens over time to the growth variable, the limiting factor, and the capacity investment in the story.

4. Fill in the blank systems archetype template with the key variables you identified. Label each arrow with an "s" or an "o," and mark any important delays.

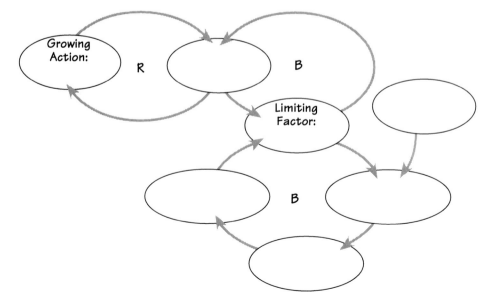

ACTIVITY 2   **YOUR OWN "GROWTH AND UNDERINVESTMENT" STORY**

INSTRUCTIONS

Follow the steps below.

STEP 1: Choose a potential "Growth and Underinvestment" situation from work, home, community, or elsewhere. The example could be about investment in individual performance (professional development, sports, physical fitness) or about organizational performance. Pick a situation that has some history so you can clearly see actual trends.

STEP 2: Make some notes about the story, enough to remind yourself of what has been happening.

STEP 3: Summarize the story in a couple of sentences. (You may find it is easier to come back to this step after you have worked with the variables and the loop diagram.)

STEP 4: List the key variables in the story.

The engine of growth:

The limiting factor(s):

The performance standard:

The needed investment:

The kind of capacity:

STEP 5: Draw the behavior over time of the engine of growth, the limiting factor, and the capacity investment.

        To confirm your graph, check with colleagues, friends, or family members to see whether your memory of the pattern of behavior matches theirs.

STEP 6: Using the "Growth and Underinvestment" causal loop template, diagram your situation. Be sure to label each arrow with an "s" or an "o," and label each loop "R" or "B."

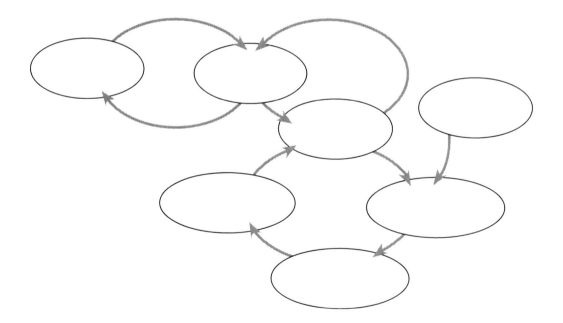

To confirm your diagram, walk through the logic of the loops. What was the growth mechanism? Did the limiting factor actually kick in? What happened when the performance gap was discovered? Was it possible to reverse the performance by investing in some kind of capacity improvement?

Then validate and broaden your insight further by showing your diagram to a friend, colleague, or family member. Remember to position the diagram as your "first-draft" attempt to understand what has been going on. Explain the diagram in terms of setting out to achieve growth, running into a limitation, and then deciding whether and how to do something about the limitation. Be sure to ask what the other person thinks and whether this explanation makes sense. Don't worry if your versions are different. Everyone's version of the story is a unique mental model, and the point is to learn more about which mental models are at work in the problems facing us.

STEP 7: What are some ways you might manage this situation of "Growth and Underinvestment"?

Notes

1. This and the following subsection are from "'Growth and Underinvestment': Is Your Company Playing with a Wooden Racket?" *Systems Archetypes I: Diagnosing Systemic Issues and Designing High-Leverage Interventions,* by Daniel H. Kim (Pegasus Communications, Inc., 1992).

2. From "Can Gateway 2000 Service Its Success?" by Daniel H. Kim and Anne Coyle, *The Systems Thinker,* Volume 4, Number 8, October 1993 (Pegasus Communications, Inc.).

Success to the Successful

In a "Success to the Successful" situation, two or more individuals, groups, projects, initiatives, etc. are vying for a limited pool of resources to achieve success. If one of them starts to become more successful (or is historically already more successful) than the others, it tends to garner more resources, thereby increasing the likelihood of continued success. Its initial success justifies devoting more resources while robbing the other alternatives of resources and opportunities to build their own success, even if the others are superior alternatives.

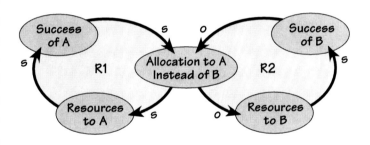

THE STORYLINE:

The Road to Success at MutualLife[1]

Chris is the group director of the capital-appreciation fund group at MutualLife, a mutual fund and insurance company. Each year, the company sponsors several internships as one way of identifying top talent for future hire. Chris has signed up to work with two interns, Alex and Terry, both of whom seem to have high potential. She feels fortunate that both might merit a job offer at the end of the internship.

She begins by giving Alex and Terry each a challenging project to work on as a way of "getting their feet wet." Both interns dive into their projects with equal zeal and appear to be doing well. During the second week, however, Terry suffers from a severe bout of intestinal flu and is out sick for a full week. Chris is genuinely understanding of the situation and reassures him that the project can wait until he recuperates. In the meantime, she is able to focus more of her attention on mentoring Alex with his project and is delighted at the progress he is making. By the time Terry returns to work and is getting himself reoriented, Alex is moving on to the next assignment.

Chris welcomes Terry back and makes a note to herself to spend more time with him once he has a chance to get back into the swing of things. Meanwhile, she continues to work intensively with Alex and enjoys the rapport they have established. As the weeks go on, she finds that time spent working with Alex pays off much more than when she spends it with Terry. When she does work with Terry, she can't help but compare his progress with Alex's, and she notices that Terry doesn't quite seem to get the hang of things.

As the internship comes to a close, Chris sadly concludes that although both had shown equal promise at first, Terry turned out not to have what it takes to make it at MutualLife. She decides to make only one job offer—to Alex. Was her assessment correct or did she lose out on hiring a candidate that was equally as good as Alex?

SELF-FULFILLING PROPHECIES: THE GENERIC STORY BEHIND "SUCCESS TO THE SUCCESSFUL"

As we saw in the story about MutualLife, when you're in the middle of a "Success to the Successful" situation, the feedback you receive reinforces the validity of your decisions to keep investing in one option rather than the other—in effect, the whole scenario becomes a self-fulfilling prophecy. After all, Chris's assessment of Alex's superior performance is supported by her experience of working with the two interns, which justifies spending more time with Alex. However, the "Success to the Successful" archetype suggests that success often depends on initial conditions and the structural forces that reinforce those initial conditions rather than on the intrinsic merits of one alternative compared to another.

The structure of this archetype forces two or more alternatives to compete for a limited resource, such as a manager's time and attention, a company's investments, or training facilities. If one of the alternatives either starts with more resources or is given more at the start (for whatever reason), that alternative has a higher likelihood of succeeding than the other(s) because of the structure of the archetype. This is because the initial success tends to justify devoting more resources to the first party and reducing investments in the second party (often with a "let's wait and see" attitude). As the second party gets fewer resources, its success diminishes, which further reinforces the "bet on the winner" approach to allocating resources.

"Success to the Successful" can thus be seen as the archetype of the self-fulfilling prophecy—by taking actions consistent with our beliefs (in the rightness of our choice), we end up creating that reality. In the MutualLife story, it could very well have been the case that if Alex had had a slower start for some reason, Terry might have pulled ahead and ended up outshining him. Either way, it may be the initial belief that one alternative is more capable or valuable than the other that drives the result.

There are three conditions that create the dynamics of a "Success to the Successful" archetype. First, there is a zero-sum game structure where two or more alternatives are vying (implicitly or explicitly) for the same resource. This means that whenever one gets more of that resource, the others are most likely to get less. The second condition is that garnering more resources does in fact help the chosen alternative to become more successful. The third condition is that the reduction of resources to the other alternative(s) accelerates its diminishing success. In the case of Alex and Terry, if Chris's attention to one had not been not linked to the other, and she had ended up focusing equally on or "catching up" with Terry, the "Success to the Successful" dynamic may not have occurred. Or, if Alex's performance hadn't improved as a function of Chris's attention or if Terry's success had not been dependent on the attention given by Chris, this archetype would not be relevant.

BEHAVIOR OVER TIME OF "SUCCESS TO THE SUCCESSFUL"

The typical pattern of behavior over time for the "Success to the Successful" archetype looks like a pair of diverging curves, one heading up and the other heading down (see Figure 7.1, "Behavior Over Time of 'Success to the Successful'"). The performance trend for the individual, product, or organization that receives resources first is represented by an upward-sloping line. The performance trend for the other person, product, or group is represented by a downward-sloping line.

FIGURE 7.1

Behavior Over Time of "Success to the Successful"

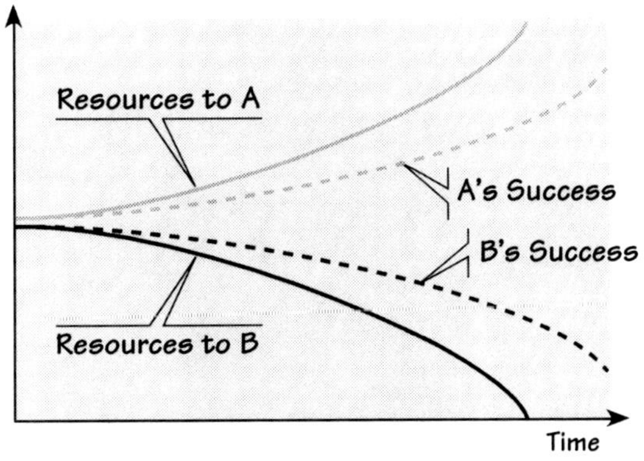

THE SYSTEMIC STRUCTURE BEHIND "SUCCESS TO THE SUCCESSFUL"

The causal loop diagram showing the systemic structure behind "Success to the Successful" consists of two reinforcing loops linked by a common variable (see Figure 7.2, "The Structure Behind 'Success to the Successful'"). This central variable—"Allocation to A Instead of B"—refers to the favoring of party A over party B; for example, the allocation of resources to A instead of B, the preference of A over B, or the belief in A over B.

As preference for A over B goes up, the energy in the system moves into the left-hand loop (R1). Resources going to A increase, which increases the success of A, which encourages continuing or even increasing allocation of resources to A.

At the same time, preference for A over B leads to *decreasing* resources for B (R2). B's success drops, or at least does not increase as much relative to A's success. This diminished success by B (relative to A) reinforces the preference to allocate resources to A. This archetype is well suited for capturing the dynamics of many political realities in organizations, such as nepotism, the "fair-haired child," and pet projects.

FIGURE 7.2

The Structure Behind "Success to the Successful"

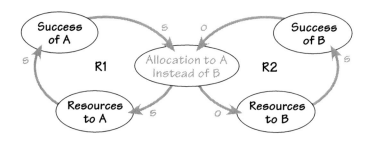

APPLYING STRUCTURE TO STORY

The MutualLife story can be retold through the lens of the "Success to the Successful" archetype (see Figure 7.3, "Success to Alex"). Because Terry is out sick, Alex gets a head start on his projects and demonstrates initial success. This head start creates a preference for Alex over Terry, which leads Chris to invest more time and attention in Alex (R3). Her attention enhances Alex's success, which leads her to prefer investing more of her time with him. When Terry returns, the reinforcing success engine for Alex has already begun. Now Chris has less time to spend with Terry, which reduces Terry's success and in turn justifies even more preference for Alex (R4).

If Terry had *not* gotten sick, several things could have occurred. One, something else might have happened to lead Chris to favor Alex over

FIGURE 7.3

Success to Alex

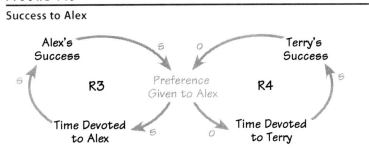

Terry. Two, something different might have led to Chris's favoring Terry over Alex. Three, Chris might have been determined to develop both as equally as possible and discovered that both were quite capable and worth hiring. In the context of limited resources, however, there is always pressure to make quick assessments about where to bet those limited resources. With supervisory time as a scarce resource, managers like Chris are likely to be susceptible to this structure, even though they may have the best of intentions when they first start out.

DIAGRAMMING "SUCCESS TO THE SUCCESSFUL"

The key to diagramming "Success to the Successful" is identifying the central variable involving choice and allocation of resources. To check that a "Success to the Successful" dynamic is really in place, confirm that the rationale for the allocation of resources does have the effect of shifting resources from one party to another. The next step is to verify that the resulting success leads to allocation of even more resources to the successful party. Finally, check that the increase or decrease of resources allocated does indeed produce increased and decreased success, respectively.

A DEEPER LOOK AT "SUCCESS TO THE SUCCESSFUL"

What can we learn from "Success to the Successful"? This archetype warns us about how resource allocation strategies can create self-fulfilling prophecies. They can also lead to *competency traps*. In a competency trap, an individual or organization becomes competent or successful through using a particular skill, tool, or product, and past success leads them to do more of the same. Past success makes change and exploration in a new area seem risky, difficult, even impossible. The longer the current success has been in place, the less the person or company is willing to risk change and see their success diminish. This dynamic illuminates another downside of the "Success to the Successful" story—we can stay trapped in the glory of our old success until that success becomes our coffin.

One of the deep operating assumptions that undergird many management decisions is the "survival of the fittest" mentality that actually encourages the kind of dynamic represented by the "Success to the Successful" structure. At this point in learning about "Success to the Successful," you might even be asking, "What's so bad about devoting resources to the best candidate, even if that means the other candidate loses out, as long as we get the end result that we want?" But therein lies the problem: How do we know that we are getting the result we want or the best result possible? The archetype tells us that we convince ourselves to be happy with the result we get, because we believe beforehand that the path we have chosen will produce the best result. That is the nature of the self-fulfilling dynamic. This archetype asks us to consider the possibility that we may be unnecessarily setting ourselves up for a win-lose outcome. For example, in the case of MutualLife, Chris may have been able to develop two good candidates for hire instead of one if she had stayed focused on both of them for that purpose. Clarifying upfront what we ultimately want to accomplish can guide us in making those resource allocation decisions better rather than allowing those decisions to be driven by assessments of relative success.

Another strong operating assumption in many organizations is captured in the saying, "Why mess with success?" Contained within this question are the seeds of the competency trap we mentioned earlier. In the short run, it almost always will seem to make more sense to invest in the current success rather than in something new. The downside of this tendency is that we will continue to use inferior tools or methods because we are so familiar with them and are unwilling to make the necessary investment to shift to a better set. This tendency can have fatal consequences when we are unable to see beyond our current competencies and fail to invest in newly emerging ones. Breaking out of competency traps also requires us to clarify what we are really trying to accomplish with the new product or initiative. We must then examine how the success of the current effort can systematically undermine support for the new initiative and find a way to decouple those decisions.

 ## Managing "Success to the Successful"

There are several guidelines that can help you examine your individual or organizational success patterns to become more aware of and manage self-fulfilling prophecies and to learn to avoid competency traps.

- **Find out how the current decision about how to allocate resources came about.**

What were the criteria for making the decision? Are they relevant now?

- **List the competencies of all the parties involved in and impacted by the allocation decision.**

Then, brainstorm about how you might use your resources differently if you broadened your allocation beyond the first, most obvious deserving party. For example, could you use a different technology? Explore a different market? Deploy people in a different way?

- **Examine the ways you currently measure your success.**

We tend to think that we believe what we measure, but it's more likely that we measure what we believe. When our measures become confirming instruments of our beliefs, they can skew our picture of how well we are doing or how attractive an alternative is.

- **Identify your internal model of success and compare it to external models.**

For example, peers, consultants, industry analysts, and competitors may shed valuable new light on what is really working in today's business environment.

- **Challenge internal resistance to innovation.**

How would you beat yourself if you were your own competitor? How would you improve your performance if you were a new coach?

- **Consider how your mental models are influencing your choices.**

When embarking on new ventures, remember that whenever we choose one thing or person over another, we need to ask what data and what mental models are shaping that choice. We can also ask whether it is possible and useful to find ways to develop more than one product line or management candidate.

- **Ask yourself, "What result am I trying to achieve?"**

Is it okay if one party in this situation succeeds and one fails? Or do you want both parties to be strong? Is our goal to preserve a current product or practice, or is it to be the most successful in the marketplace?

IN SUMMARY

"Success to the Successful" raises questions about what drives success in certain situations. It shows how small differences in initial conditions can have powerful long-term effects on the outcome. It's analogous to the butterfly effect in chaos science, where the flapping of a single butterfly's wings can be the cause of a hurricane hundreds of miles away. This archetype points out that small (perhaps random) variations at the beginning of a process can end up determining the final outcome if we are not clear about the overall result we are trying to achieve. It also points out how we can convince ourselves to stay trapped in old lines of business or outmoded ways of doing things because we are already "good" at it.

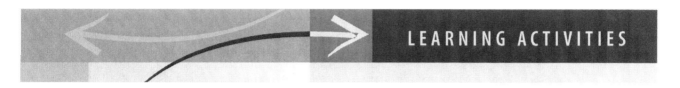

LEARNING ACTIVITIES

Now that you've learned about "Success to the Successful," you might want to try your hand at the Learning Activities below. These exercises will give you an opportunity to identify a "Success to the Successful" dynamic in a story, and to examine a "Success to the Successful" story from your own experience.

In each Learning Activity, you will be asked to provide:

• A statement of the theme of the story

• A list of key variables

• A graph of the key variables' distinctive behavior over time

• A causal loop diagram of the systemic structure generating the "Success to the Successful" situation.

After completing the Learning Activities below, compare your responses with those in Appendix A. Don't worry if your responses look different from the ones in the appendix; there's no one right "answer" in a systems thinking analysis. These activities are mainly meant to get you thinking about the themes, patterns of behavior, and systemic structure of the archetypes.

ACTIVITY 1   HOOKED ON TECHNOLOGY

The Story ➤ Update, Inc., a newsletter publisher, wants to stay current with the latest publishing technology. As the company begins exploring options, the manager of the corporate communications department purchases two leading desktop-publishing software packages. The publications editor is very excited about learning *PubExpress.* She takes her group to a week-long training, and they begin trying out the new software immediately.

As more internal publishing assignments come in, corporate communications hires three new staff members. Two of them have used the other publishing software, *DeskTop.* However, because staff members need to be able to exchange files and work on each other's projects, the newcomers' recommendations that the company switch to *DeskTop* are not pursued.

When upgrades are offered, the manager chooses *PubExpress 4.2* and later *5.0.* If anyone points out the superiority of *DeskTop,* the manager reminds them of the investment of time, money, and training in *PubExpress* that Update has already put in. One day, the staff hears rumors that a large software company might buy the rights to *DeskTop* and incorporate it into a new operating system plus desktop-publishing package. What to do?

INSTRUCTIONS

1. Summarize the "Success to the Successful" theme in this story in two or three sentences.

2. Identify the key variables in the story.

   The resource allocation variable is _____.

   This allocation rationale leads to an increase in _____, which leads to an increase in _____.

   The allocation rationale also leads to a decrease in _____, which leads to less _____.

3. Graph what happens over time to usage of the two software packages.

4. Fill in the blank systems archetype template below with the variables you identified. Label each arrow with an "s" or an "o."

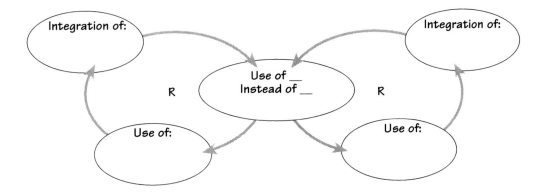

ACTIVITY 2   **YOUR OWN "SUCCESS TO THE SUCCESSFUL" STORY**

INSTRUCTIONS

Follow the steps below.

STEP 1: Choose a potential "Success to the Successful" situation from work, home, community, or elsewhere. Pick one that has some history so you can clearly see actual trends.

STEP 2: Make some notes about the story, enough to remind yourself of what has been happening.

STEP 3: Summarize the story in a couple of sentences. (You may find it is easier to come back to this step after you have worked with the variables and the loop diagram.)

STEP 4: List the key variables in the story.

The central variable:

The successful loop variables:

The unsuccessful loop variables:

STEP 5: Graph the behavior over time of the resources allocated and the success of each party in your situation. To confirm your graph, check with colleagues, friends, or family members to see whether your memory of the pattern of behavior matches theirs.

STEP 6: Using the "Success to the Successful" causal loop template, diagram your situation. Remember to label each arrow with an "s" or an "o," and label each loop "R" or "B."

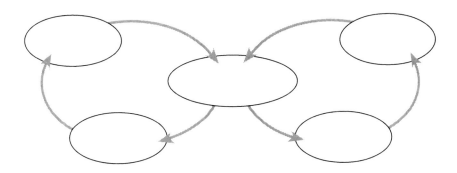

To confirm your diagram, walk through the logic of the loops. Looking at the successful and unsuccessful dynamic, does the allocation variable make sense? Have you accurately reflected the successful dynamic and the unsuccessful one?

Validate and broaden your insights further by showing your diagram to a friend, colleague, or family member. Remember to position the diagram as your "first-draft" attempt to understand what has been going on. Explain the diagram in terms of the decision to favor or invest in one party over another and then the divergent outcomes. Be sure to ask what the other person thinks and whether this explanation makes sense. Don't worry if your versions are different. Everyone's version of the story is a unique mental model, and the point is to learn more about which mental models are at work in the problems facing us.

STEP 7: Do you think there were or are alternatives to the way allocation decisions were made in the situation you described? Do you see any competency traps? What would it take for different choices to be made in this situation?

Notes

1. This and the following subsection are adapted from "'Success to the Successful': Self-Fulfilling Prophecies," *Systems Archetypes I: Diagnosing Systemic Issues and Designing High-Leverage Intervnetions,* by Daniel H. Kim (Pegasus Communications, Inc., 1992).

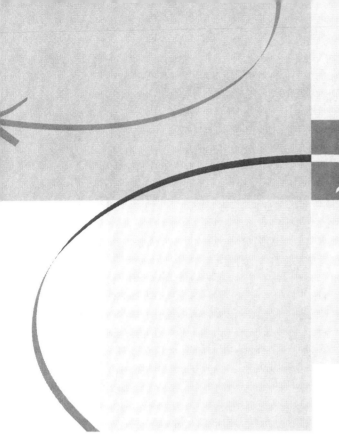

Escalation

In an "Escalation" situation, one party (A) takes actions to counter a perceived threat. These actions are then perceived by the other party (B) as creating an imbalance in the system that then makes them feel threatened. So, B responds to close the gap, creating an imbalance from A's perspective, and on it goes. The dynamic of two parties, each trying to achieve a sense of "safety," becomes an overall reinforcing process that escalates tension on both sides, tracing a figure-8 pattern with the two balancing loops in this archetype.

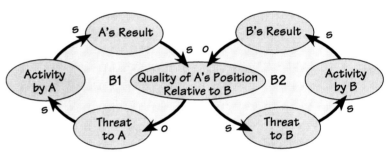

THE STORYLINE:

Cosmic Versus Universal Air

It's the typical story of yet another price war among rival airlines. Cosmic Air wants to fill more of the empty seats on their flights, so they cut their fares. As passengers respond to the bargain fares, Universal Air finds their bookings declining and counters with an even more attractive discount offer. Cosmic, in turn, creates another special promotion, offering a "two for the price of one" deal to customers. In the short run, travelers benefit from the low prices, but in the long term, everyone *could* lose—and lose big. Depressed prices mean that the profitability of both airlines involved in the price war suffers. As a result, they have less funds to invest in equipment, maintenance, staff, and training—a dangerous situation for them *and* their customers.

A LOSE-LOSE SITUATION: THE GENERIC STORY BEHIND "ESCALATION"[1]

You may have seen or been involved in a situation where a minor incident quickly escalated into a major blowout before anyone even knew what was happening. Perhaps it's a little disagreement at a meeting that turns into an interdepartmental war. Or, it begins as a trivial problem with your teenager that blows up into a shouting match. Or, it's one country's efforts to build "defensive" weapons that leads another to build their own, which turns into the biggest arms race in human history.

In a way, all of these situations are not too unlike how schoolyard fights get started. This image of a schoolyard fight captures the essence of the "Escalation" archetype: One kid makes a pejorative comment that the other counters with a sharp rebuttal. The next round of remarks is even louder and more entrenched. Each side sticks his neck out farther and farther; sometimes the onlookers even seem to egg on the mounting hostilities. Pretty soon, both sides are so far out on a limb that you can almost imagine the playground chant: "Fight! Fight! Fight!" Once things have reached a fever pitch, it is hard to see how anyone will be able to climb down from their positions.

"Escalation" dynamics thrive in a competitive environment, so—not surprisingly—they are pervasive in business. The usual logic that drives "Escalation" goes something like this: Whenever your competitor gains, you lose, and vice versa. That logic leads to all kinds of "wars"—price wars, advertising contests, rebate and promotion slug-fests, salary and benefits wars, labor vs. management conflicts, marketing vs. manufacturing department battles, and so on. And in the end, everyone loses. Yet the dynamic can also work in a positive direction, when the parties induce each other to compete to *improve* a situation. The challenge in any "Escalation" situation is to find a way to turn it around so that it leads to good things for all the parties involved, rather than a downward spiral of destruction.

 ## BEHAVIOR OVER TIME OF "ESCALATION"

There are several distinctive patterns of behavior over time generated by "Escalation." A graph depicting the "Escalation" of activity by both parties would show parallel upward-curving lines. In some cases, dominance shifts between the two parties. A graph showing that level of detail would contain a pair of lines that twine or zigzag across each other (see Figure 8.1, "Behavior Over Time of Escalating Activity").

A graph of an "Escalation" dynamic can also be summarized by a single line representing the overall trend in a variable, such as each party's "sense of being right" (between individuals or departments) or prices (in a price war) (see Figure 8.2, "Behavior Over Time of 'Escalation' Trends"). In the first instance, the individuals' overall perceived sense of being right trends upward; in the second, prices trend downward.

FIGURE 8.1

Behavior Over Time of Escalating Activity

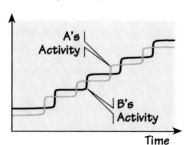

FIGURE 8.2

Behavior Over Time of "Escalation" Trends

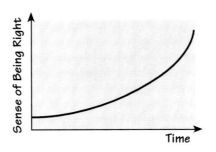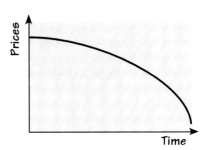

FIGURE 8.3

Combining "Escalation" Graphs

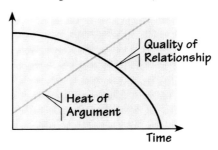

Finally, an "Escalation" graph could combine both the rising and falling trends generated by the dynamic (see Figure 8.3, "Combining 'Escalation' Graphs").

 ## THE SYSTEMIC STRUCTURE BEHIND "ESCALATION"

At the heart of an "Escalation" dynamic are two or more parties, each of whom feels threatened by the actions of the other. Each side attempts to improve their own situation by managing their own balancing process (see Figure 8.4, "The Structure Behind 'Escalation'"). The result is that both sides keep ratcheting up the action as each perceives the other gaining an advantage.

FIGURE 8.4

The Structure Behind "Escalation"

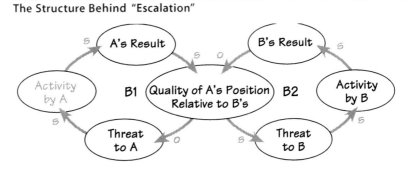

If we start following the dynamic of this structure in the left-hand loop of Figure 8.4, we see that when A takes actions by increasing its activity, the quality of A's position relative to B goes up (B1). A then feels better about its position relative to B and slows down its activity. As a result of A's actions, however, B now feels more threatened by A and increases its activity, improving its results and its relative position over A (B2). As B feels it is gaining the "upper hand" over A, we're back to A feeling threatened again . . . and the "Escalation" cycle takes another spin around both loops.

➤ APPLYING STRUCTURE TO STORY

In the airline price wars story, Cosmic cuts its prices first in an effort to increase its market share (see Figure 8.5, "Cosmic Versus Universal Air"). Cosmic's sales increase, and so does its market share relative to Universal's (B3). Universal feels threatened by Cosmic's price reductions and apparent success, and responds with its own price cuts (B4). Universal's sales go up, eroding Cosmic's market-share gains. If Cosmic wants to "play hardball," it comes back with even more price cuts. And so it goes, until something stops the cycle: Customers quit responding to further cuts, the airlines can't afford to cut any lower, or someone goes out of business.

➤ DIAGRAMMING AN "ESCALATION" STORY

The key to diagramming an "Escalation" structure is identifying the central variable that links the health or comfort level of one party with that

FIGURE 8.5

Cosmic Versus Universal Air

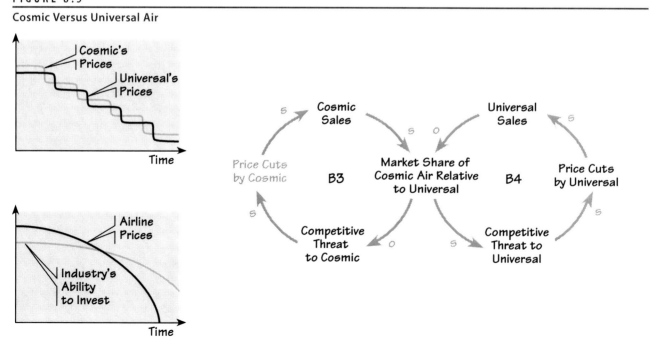

of another. Once you have clarified what the escalation is all about, identify who took what set of actions that initiated the escalation. After doing that, you can then work on identifying the sequence of threat, action, and results—on both sides—that keeps tipping the balance of power from one side to the other.

 ## A Deeper Look at "Escalation"

When two (or sometimes more) parties get intensely involved in reacting to each other's actions, the resulting dynamics are hard to miss. But there are several other less obvious aspects of this structure that deserve a bit more attention. Specifically, we can think of "Escalation" as consisting of two balancing structures that work together like the dual ends of a see-saw—the harder you push up at one end of the see-saw, the harder the other end has to work to absorb the momentum. Notice that the two balancing loops are like mirror images in which the direction of movement branching away from the central variable is opposite in the two loops. For example, when the quality of A's position relative to B goes down, A's sense of threat goes *up.* (Note the "o" link between "Quality of A's Position Relative to B" and "Threat to A.") However, when the quality of A's position relative to B goes up, B's sense of threat also goes *up.* (Note the "s" link.) The result of such a competitive coupling of these two balancing loops is that the *overall* dynamic produced is a reinforcing cycle. As each party tries to gain the upper hand, their relationship or the condition of their industry tends to worsen. The interaction of the two parties trying to "stay alive," get ahead, or hold onto what they have produces a reinforcing spiral in which nobody feels in control. If you "untwist" the two loops from their figure-8 connection, a single reinforcing loop emerges (see Figure 8.6, "Untwisting the Figure-8").

Another interesting thing to note about "Escalation" is the way it demonstrates the power of our mental models to create our reality. This structure shows how we can think that a threat is present, then act to

FIGURE 8.6

Untwisting the Figure-8

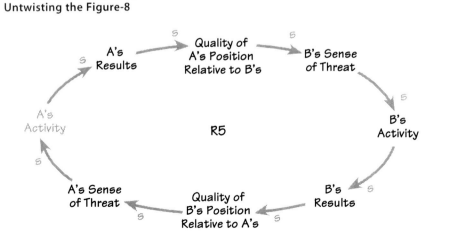

defend ourselves against it, and by those very actions *produce* the threatening behavior that we originally feared. Our fears become our reality. The irony is that even as *we create* this reality, it can look to us as if the threat is happening *to* us.

A third aspect of this dynamic to note is that, as a structure, "Escalation" has the potential to produce either a negative or a positive result for all parties involved. So far, we've described mostly the dynamics of "Escalation" that produce negative results; however, this archetype can also be the story of escalating rounds of improved performance, quality, or capability. That is, we can drive any escalation structure in reverse.

The speed with which the dominance shifts from loop to loop can also vary dramatically. In the case of a price war or a negotiation, it may take a day or a week for the action to move through both loops, while in an arms race between countries, the dynamics may unfold over a period of many years. In an argument, on the other hand, the dynamics can race through both loops in a matter of seconds, as emotions run wild.

One last thing to note is that, in some situations, the escalating structure leads people to ratchet up their defenses/offenses in advance, as they anticipate one another's moves and prepare their second and third rebuttals or price moves before the other party has even made an initial move. Anticipation can accelerate the dynamic as we project onto others motives and actions that we know "those kind of people" will take. This serves to reinforce mental models about the other players that makes stopping the "Escalation" simply unthinkable.

 ## Managing "Escalation"

As an old saying goes, it takes two to have an argument (or a price war), but only one to stop it. This is good news for those who genuinely want to halt this dynamic, because unilateral action can break "Escalation" and rob it of its legitimacy. If one side stops arguing or lowering prices, the source of the threat diminishes, giving the other party less reason to keep arguing or lowering prices. Such unilateral "disarmament" can actually cause the structure to run in reverse. If one party changes its mental model of the situation, the other may follow suit, and the entire scenario can transform into a positive development.

In the heat of battle, a company can get locked into one competitive variable, such as price, and neglect to emphasize other strengths. The escalation dynamic "sucks them in" and they become myopically focused on that one thing. In this archetype, more than the others, emotions end up playing a big role in driving the dynamics. For example, in the case of Texas Instruments (TI) and the 99/4A computer, even though TI had a technically superior product, they got caught up in a price war with Commodore and lost. Instead of focusing on features that outgunned Commodore, they were pulled into a price war that they could not win, because Commodore's product was significantly cheaper to make. In the end, TI had to write off its entire personal computer business, costing the company hundreds of millions of dollars.

In situations where the variable of focus is the only (or primary) factor distinguishing the parties, reversing or stopping the escalation can be difficult. For example, in the short run, it is difficult for either Cosmic or Universal to respond to a price cut by emphasizing some other aspect of their service. In the absence of other distinguishing features, the market is generally very sensitive to price. In the short term, the best each company can do is to try to keep things from going out of control by matching rather than exceeding the other's actions. In the long term, however, the way to be less susceptible to this structure is to develop other ways in which your product or service stands apart from others.

If you suspect that you may be caught in an "Escalation" dynamic, drawing out the archetype may help you gain a better perspective. The following questions may be useful for identifying and defusing an "Escalation" dynamic:

- Who are the parties whose actions are perceived as threats?

- What is being threatened, and what is the source of that threat?

- What are the relative measures pitting one party against the other— and can they be changed?

- What are the deep-rooted assumptions beneath the actions taken in response to the threat?

- What are the significant delays in the system that may distort the true nature of the threat?

- At what speed does the sense of threat activate the system, and is anticipation at work?

- How do speed and anticipation make slowing down or stopping more difficult?

- What is a larger goal that might encompass the individual goals and move the dynamic to another playing field?

In highly competitive industries and businesses, it may be impossible to completely avoid "Escalation" structures. In some cases, when it serves to elevate everyone's performance through "friendly competition," "Escalation" can be exciting and stimulating: Which team can reduce errors more than anyone else? Who can achieve the better safety record? In such cases, the dynamics wouldn't be driven by threat, but rather by actions that keep raising the standard of performance for the other. In a way, that is the best outcome of competition—each bringing out the best in the other through higher and higher levels of play.

The following suggestions contain some pointers for identifying and avoiding destructive cases of "Escalation":

- Watch out for commoditization, where price is the only differentiating factor, or when all competition is focused on only one visible dimension.

- Look for areas of competition that are harder to quantify or have "wars" about, or where escalation could actually be healthy—such as reinforcing cycles of ever-increasing quality, reliability, or safety.

- Within your organization, clearly establish the overarching objective of all the efforts, and make sure that any escalation among groups is in service of the larger goal. For example, two groups may be set up to create the best next-generation product. In such a case, make sure that the competing structure leads to overall cooperation to achieve the ultimate purpose (design the best product for the company) and not to destructive competition where the goal becomes "beat the other team."

- Examine assumptions about the zero-sum game within your organization. Make sure that your reward and incentive systems are not set up in a way that encourages destructive escalation behaviors.

 ## In Summary

As the term *threat* suggests, the "Escalation" structure is often about insecurity. Arguing for the sake of being right may stem from each person's or group's insecurity about identity or status. Engaging in a price war may be a symptom of each airline's insecurity about its ability to attract customers on a basis other than price.

A little objectivity can help us bring feelings of insecurity under control. Slowing down to consider how the "Escalation" structure is working, and to examine the mental models that drive it, can provide this objectivity and a wider perspective on the dynamic. Mapping our situation onto this archetype can help us to see the larger, longer-term negative consequence of a short-term reaction that, on its surface, may seem reasonable. Examining assumptions and mental models that we hold about the other players can also open up possible alternative explanations and paths of action that can lead to de-escalation or a virtuous escalation.

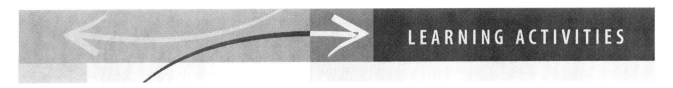

LEARNING ACTIVITIES

Now that you've learned about "Escalation," try your hand at the Learning Activities below. These exercises will give you an opportunity to identify an "Escalation" dynamic in a story, and to analyze an "Escalation" story from your own experience.

In each Learning Activity, you will be asked to provide:

- A statement of the theme of the story
- A list of key variables
- A graph of the key variables' distinctive behavior over time
- A causal loop diagram of the systemic structure generating the "Escalation" situation.

After completing the Learning Activities below, compare your responses with those in Appendix A. Don't worry if your responses look different from the ones in the appendix; there's no one right "answer" in a systems thinking analysis. These activities are mainly meant to get you thinking about the themes, patterns of behavior, and systemic structure of the archetypes.

Activity 1　　　　　　　　　　　　　　　　　　　　　**ESCALATING BENEFITS**

The Story ➤　In an area known as "Little Silicon Valley," there are a number of growing high-tech companies continually on the lookout to hire capable new college graduates. However, the population of people in their 20s has been shrinking over the years, forcing the companies to compete for an ever-shrinking pool of top talent.

The "benefit boom" starts when ElCo decides to get aggressive about attracting recruits. Its first move is to sweeten its benefit package for new hires with additional vacation time and a stock-option plan. Hiring improves at ElCo, while the company's main rival, DataTech, continues to struggle to find good prospects. So the next fall, DataTech enhances its own benefits package by adding education-loan assistance, as well as new standard vacation and stock-option plans. By Thanksgiving, they have filled their open positions, while ElCo is still running ads.

Over the next 18 months, the two companies take turns improving their respective benefits packages, and after each round, they find that the "standard package" of the other company has been ratcheted up. Then one day, the human-resources director at DataTech discovers that ElCo is offering a better benefit package and a bonus for individuals with a high-performance track record at *another competing company*. The director sputters, "That does it—something has to be done!"

INSTRUCTIONS

1. Summarize the "Escalation" theme in this story in two or three sentences.

2. Identify the key variables in the story.

    The central variable is _____.

    The threat is _____.

    The initiating action taken is _____.

    The result is _____.

3. Graph what happens over time to the central variable.

4. Fill in the blank systems archetype below with the variables you identified. Label each arrow with an "s" or an "o."

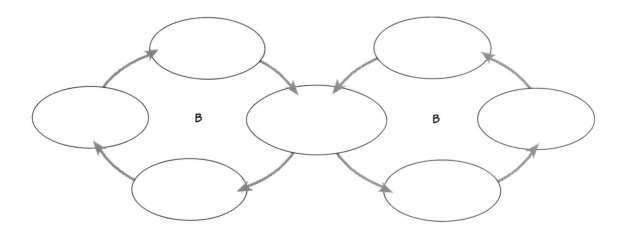

5. What could DataTech do to de-escalate this situation?

ACTIVITY 2 **YOUR OWN "ESCALATION" STORY**

INSTRUCTIONS

STEP 1: Choose a possible "Escalation" situation from work, home, community, or elsewhere. Pick one that has some history so you can clearly see actual trends and the impact of actual interventions.

STEP 2: Make some notes about the story, enough to remind yourself of what has been happening.

STEP 3: Summarize the story in a couple of sentences. (You may find it is easier to come back to this step after you have worked with the variables and the loop diagram.)

STEP 4: List the key variables in the story. If your initial list is quite long (more than six or seven variables), try aggregating some of them or narrowing the focus of the story.

Central variable:

Threat:

Initiating action taken:

Result:

STEP 5: Draw the pattern of behavior over time of the central variable. Check with colleagues, friends, or family members to see whether your memory of the pattern of behavior matches theirs.

STEP 6: Using the "Escalation" causal loop template below, diagram your situation. Label each arrow with an "s" or an "o," and each loop with a "B" or an "R."

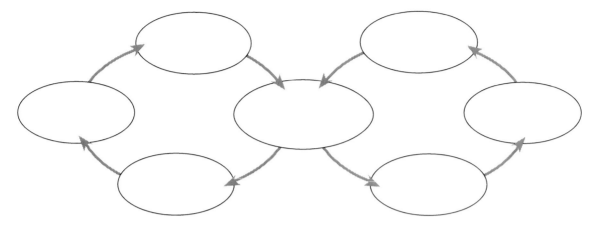

To confirm your diagram, walk through the logic of the loops. Is the central variable the need that drives the two parties to compete? Will the results actually satisfy that need? Does the action taken produce those results? Does the dynamic fluctuate back and forth between the two parties, like a tennis volley?

Validate and broaden your insight further by showing your diagram to a friend, colleague, or family member. Remember to position the diagram as your "first-draft" attempt to understand what has been going on. Explain the diagram in terms of the competition between the two parties over the central variable. Then be sure to ask the other person what he or she thinks and whether your explanation makes sense. Don't worry if your versions are different. Everyone's version of the story is a unique mental model, and the point is to learn more about which mental models are at work in the problems facing us.

STEP 7: What do you think it would take to de-escalate the situation you chose? What would it have taken at the beginning of the situation to avoid the "Escalation" altogether?

Notes

1. This and the next subsection, as well as the subsection on managing "Escalation" on p. 104, are adapted from "'Escalation': The Dynamics of Insecurity," *Systems Archetypes I: Diagnosing Systemic Issues and Designing High-Leverage Interventions,* by Daniel H. Kim (Pegasus Communications, Inc., 1992).

Tragedy of the Commons

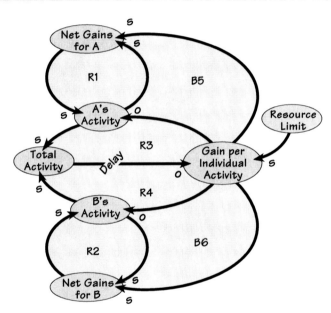

In a "Tragedy of the Commons" situation, individuals make use of a common resource by pursuing actions for their own enjoyment or benefit, without concern for the collective impact of everyone's actions. At some point, the sum of all individual activity overloads the "commons," and all parties involved experience diminishing benefits. The commons may even collapse.

THE STORYLINE:

Too Many Boats Chasing Too Few Fish[1]

Over one-third of the world's fisheries monitored by the United Nations' Food & Agriculture Organization (FAO) are currently being overfished or have already been depleted. This realization has prompted action on two fronts. Several countries have agreed to stop fishing for certain species for periods of time. Meanwhile, governments are working to lay the foundation for better long-term management of the fisheries. However, there have also been incidents of threats, armed violence, and poaching—clearly, the stakes are high. The FAO estimates that worldwide overfishing and poor management have lowered the short-term potential for optimum revenues from fishing by at least $15 billion a year. Too many boats chasing too few fish have kept the world fleet operating at a loss, despite enormous annual subsidies.

How have things reached this point? Each fisherman, each nation's fishing fleet, heads out to sea to net as many fish as they can. As long as the worldwide fishing fleet doesn't harvest the fish faster than they can regenerate themselves, the situation is fine. And for centuries, the overall supply of fish has been more than adequate. During the 20th century, however, the growing markets for fish and the growing capacity of fishermen to harvest the seas at an ever-increasing rate has led to situations where the fish are being caught faster than they can regenerate. That is, the supply of available fish has been shrinking in some areas.

In the face of diminishing harvests, each fisherman naturally increases his efforts in order to make up for the shortfall. This strategy seems to work in the short run: The harder the fishermen work, the more fish they catch. However, the situation becomes worse in the long run, because the fish supply gets depleted even further, making each trip out to sea more and more difficult and less and less productive. To compensate, some fishermen may invest in better boats, better nets, and the latest fish-finding technology. Again, the results improve in the short run, only to worsen as the fish supply gets depleted even further.

Many cod and salmon fishermen and Gulf shrimpers have experienced exactly this dynamic, with each fisherman, each fishing fleet, catching fewer and smaller fish per trip. They have tried to compensate by staying out longer, going out farther, fishing for more days—but the ever-dwindling catch has forced many of them to abandon the industry altogether while others are observing mandated moratoria.

"All for One and None for All": The Generic Story Behind "Tragedy of the Commons"[2]

The "Tragedy of the Commons" structure is a complex, multiplayer variation on the basic "Limits to Success" story. Individual parties focus on their own objectives—for example, growing their private enterprises—which depend on a common resource such as land, air, water, plant or animal life, and minerals. Or sometimes the parties depend on a less tangible or other sort of common resource—for example, the word-processing pool, the IT support group, machine capacity, power supply, total market, or funds available for investment. In all "Tragedy of the Commons" cases, the common resource is not owned or managed by a specific individual or group. The commons is considered to be open and freely available to all.

Each player in the system discovers that they can gain from utilizing the commons without having to pay anything in return. The more they utilize it, the more they gain from their activity. So to maximize their individual benefit, they continue to take advantage of the commons as much as they want. For a period of time, which could be anywhere from months to centuries, the total activity or total draw on the resource from all players stays within the carrying capacity or limits of the commons. If the total activity never reaches the capacity limit, then the "Tragedy of the Commons" structure never gets triggered. In a world of finite resources, however, we eventually begin to hit the limits when total usage continues to grow.

As individuals notice a drop-off in their gains per effort expended—fewer fish in the nets, more time for prototypes to be completed, more mistakes in the documents—participants often respond by doubling their efforts. They may try to get to the commons faster, initiate more demands on the commons, or just outright grab more of the commons before others get to it. Of course, these kinds of tactics are quickly copied by everyone else, which further accelerates the depletion of the commons. Left unmanaged, these kinds of actions will drive the resource into collapse.

BEHAVIOR OVER TIME IN "TRAGEDY OF THE COMMONS"

The generic pattern of behavior over time for the "Tragedy of the Commons" archetype consists of three trend lines (see Figure 9.1, "Behavior Over Time in 'Tragedy of the Commons'"). One line plots the variable named Total Activity, which represents the sum of all the individual parties' efforts and results. Another line (Common Resource) tracks the level of the resource itself, while a third line (Gain per Activity) shows the gains per activity for everyone using the commons.

There are three distinct phases to the timeline that are significant in a "Tragedy of the Commons" situation. In all cases, we start out in the stable phase, where the total activity is small relative to the resources available. During this stage, an increase in activity does not decrease the gains, and people are not aware that limits may exist. This can go on indefinitely, as long as our consumption rate is slower than the commons' regeneration rate (for example, we cut down fewer trees than are planted, demand less overtime hours than employees' rejuvenation rate, etc.).

When our consumption becomes greater than the commons' replacement rate, we enter the phase of gradual decline. Here, the common

FIGURE 9.1

Behavior Over Time in "Tragedy of the Commons"

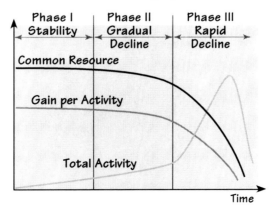

resource level begins to drop imperceptibly at first, but with greater velocity as total use of the resource accelerates. In this phase, the growth in activity is largely fueled by the increasing popularity of the resource, both among current users as well as new ones.

At some point, the consumption reaches a level such that it *affects the regeneration rate itself.* In other words, not only are we consuming faster than the commons' replacement rate, our consumption is actually causing the replacement rate to *decrease* —which means that the resource will get depleted at an even faster rate. When this happens, we have entered the third and final phase of rapid decline, which is the precursor to a total collapse of the commons if dramatic corrective actions are not taken. In this phase, the total activity is heavily influenced by the growing scarcity of the resource (which shows up in the precipitous decline in Gain per Activity). This development can lead to panicked consumption (the "I've got to get my share before it's all gone" herd mentality). Total activity grows superexponentially and then drops sharply as the commons collapses.

THE SYSTEMIC STRUCTURE BEHIND "TRAGEDY OF THE COMMONS"

Both "Limits to Success" and "Tragedy of the Commons" situations are affected by limits, but they differ in an important way. In "Limits to Success," the limits encountered are ones that could be expanded through judicious planning and timely investments in the resource. The primary lesson of "Limits to Success" is about balancing *capacity investments* and growing demand in a timely way so that future growth is not hindered by inadequate capacity. In "Tragedy of the Commons," the limits are considered "fixed" during the relevant timeframe of interest. The primary lesson of this archetype is about *managing consumption* of the resource in a way that never allows the system to enter that third phase of rapid decline.

The "Tragedy of the Commons" structure deserves special attention because it represents a "macro" view of a dynamic produced by lots of individual actors at a "micro" level. The activities of actors A and B are representative of dozens or thousands of individual actors each enjoying the benefits of using the common resource. (See Figure 9.2, "The Structure Behind 'Tragedy of the Commons,'" and note that this diagram differs from other presentations of this archetype that you may have seen—it makes explicit two new loops, R3 and R4, that were implicit in previous versions.) As each player enjoys the benefits of the activity, there is a tendency to increase the activity level, because gains increase without a proportionate increase in costs (R1 and R2). In addition, the number of participants is likely to increase as others hear about the gains to be had. Both of these tendencies accelerate the increase in the total activity level, which will eventually lead to a decrease in gain per individual activity.

FIGURE 9.2

The Structure Behind "Tragedy of the Commons"

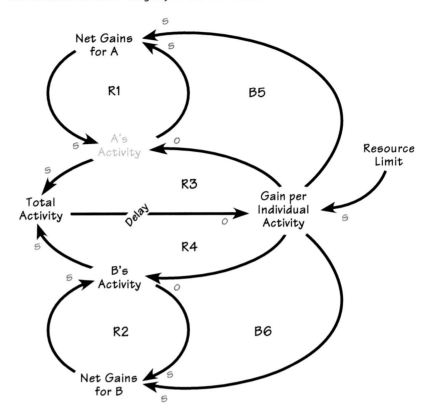

Now, if this were a "self-correcting" system, the outside balancing loops would kick in (see Figure 9.3, "Two Competing Forces," on p. 116). With a rise in total activity, gains per individual activity would eventually drop. This drop would translate into a decrease in individual gains (B5), leading to a *decrease* in individual activity and hence total activity. This would in turn eventually lead to an *increase* in gain per individual activity. Unfortunately, the setup of this archetype encourages people to do exactly the opposite—to increase their activities in response to a drop in individual gains, in the belief that they can compensate for the diminishing gains with greater efforts (R3). This strategy does appear to pay off in the short run—but only as long as we stay in phase II as shown in Figure 9.1. The sad fact, however, is that the dynamic often continues into phase III: rapid decline.

Even without the "acceleration" dynamic, the "Tragedy of the Commons" archetype has a propensity for overshoot and collapse because of the delay between when the total activity level has risen beyond a sustainable level and when that feedback shows up in the way of diminishing returns for individual users of the commons. By the time those indicators do show up, there is so much momentum in the consumption activity that it is extremely difficult to get anyone involved in the system to voluntarily reduce their activity.

FIGURE 9.3

Two Competing Forces

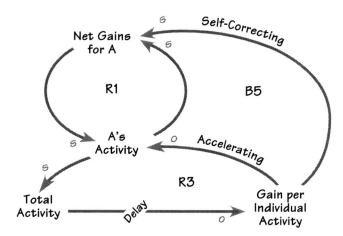

TWO COMPETING FORCES:

When gain per individual activity decreases, there are two possible paths—self-correcting and accelerating—for the energy to move through the system.

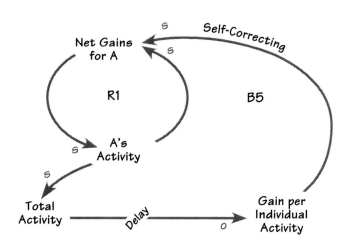

SELF-CORRECTING DYNAMICS:

When gain per individual activity decreases, this path sends the self-correcting signal to *decrease* individual and then total activity.

R1 goes in a *decreasing* reinforcing spiral until the system recovers and begins to yield higher gains.

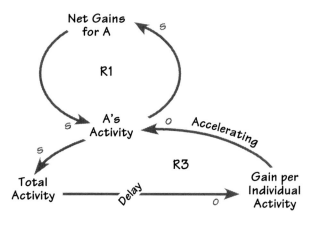

ACCELERATED DEPLETION DYNAMICS:

When gain per individual activity decreases, this path encourages individuals to compensate for the loss by *increasing* individual activity.

R1 goes in an *increasing* reinforcing spiral until the resource is completely depleted.

Applying Structure to Story

We can view the "Too Many Boats Chasing Too Few Fish" story through the "Tragedy of the Commons" "lens" to make the causal relationships driving the behavior more explicit (see Figure 9.4, "The Fisheries Problem"). Initially, each fisherman reaps increasing benefits the more effort he puts into fishing (R7 and R8). As the total number of fish caught continues to rise, the available fish starts to decline when the catch rate exceeds the regeneration rate. This means that for an equal amount of fishing effort, each individual fisherman's catch per trip also declines.

Now, here's how delay plays a critical role in what happens when the catch starts to decline. If you had just started your fishing career and had not yet invested a whole lot of time and effort, you may be more likely to abandon it when the catch per trip starts failing to cover the bills (B9 and B10). If, on the other hand, you've been fishing for quite a while and have a lot invested (boats, fishing equipment, pride, employees), you'll likely feel pressured to do what it takes to increase your catch (R11 and R12). (You might think of loops R7 and R8 as big flywheels that have been spinning for a long time—they have a lot of momentum that will keep them spinning even if the braking actions of loops B9 and B10 are applied.) Hence, the fishing continues until the catch per trip gets so bad that more and more people are forced out of the business.

The key lesson of this archetype is that, if left to the individual players to manage on their own, the commons will inevitably be destroyed.

FIGURE 9.4

The Fisheries Problem

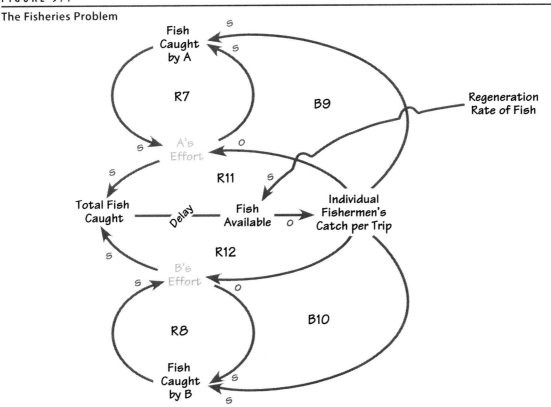

That's because, as a structure, there is no incentive for any one individual to change his or her behavior. The solution requires a collective agreement, as well as a commitment from each individual to abide by that agreement.

DIAGRAMMING "TRAGEDY OF THE COMMONS"

Although a "Tragedy of the Commons" causal loop diagram looks complex because it represents multiple players, it is basically a combination of two simpler loop structures that are mirror images of each other. The easiest approach to diagramming one of these situations is to focus on just the actions of player A and then just duplicate the loops for player B. It will feel less daunting to draw a three-loop structure instead of a six-loop one.

Begin by identifying the reinforcing loop that drives player A to want to continue his or her particular activity. Then think about what common resource might be strained if a lot of people did the same thing that A is doing. This line of thinking should lead you to identify the common resource that everyone is drawing on.

The next task is to connect the individual reinforcing actions in a way that shows the cumulative impact on the common resource. Individual activity increases total activity, which in turn ends up producing diminishing returns of some kind. Now think about how the players respond to the diminishing returns, and map both the remaining reinforcing and balancing links.

Even though the actual scenario includes many more players than just two, the causal loop diagram will become very large and busy if you try to depict all of them. Unless it is critical to your communication process to identify each player by name, limit yourself to the two-player version of the picture.

A DEEPER LOOK AT "TRAGEDY OF THE COMMONS"

To detect a "Tragedy of the Commons" situation in action, look for two key factors: a common resource that two or more players have relatively free and equal access to, and the absence of any overall oversight or management responsibility of a single governing authority.

The key challenge in a "Tragedy of the Commons" situation is coming to collective agreement on exactly what common resource is being overburdened, and on what to do about the overuse. If no one sees how his or her individual action will eventually reduce everyone's benefits, the level of debate is likely to revolve around why player B thinks that player A should stop doing what she is doing and why it's okay for player B to keep doing what he is doing. Chances are that there may be endless debates about one course of action or another, but little actually changes.

This is because the leverage for producing a solution does not lie at the individual actor level. Here's why: Suppose fisherman A decides to reduce his level of fishing because he sees that overfishing is reducing the size of the catch. What happens? Fisherman A loses because he's not getting as much fish, and the overfishing continues because that opens up more opportunity for the other fishermen to fish. As long as the system is designed to provide immediate individual gain without a way to make the long-term collective pain more evident, the players will pursue actions that maximize current benefits.

MANAGING "TRAGEDY OF THE COMMONS"[3]

Once you've identified a "Tragedy of the Commons" structure at work and have obtained agreement on the common resource, you might try this series of steps to slow down or stop the overusage and reverse or prevent the potential crash.

- Identify the motivators that drive the individual reinforcing processes. What gains is each player working to make? What motivates him or her, both externally and internally?

- Determine the time frame in which the players realize their gains. This cycle time lets you estimate the rate at which the common resource is being used. Generally, the faster the cycle of effort and reward, the higher the motivation is to use the resource and the harder it is to persuade the players to give up their short-term gains.

- Determine the time frame for depleting the resource, both the total time frame and the time remaining between now and the collapse of the resource. Now you can figure out the time frame for taking action and what kind of action you may need to take. Keep in mind, however, that because joint awareness is critical to any favorable outcome in this dynamic, *all* players in the system need to acknowledge the problem and agree on necessary actions—a difficult thing to achieve.

- One leverage point in managing a "Tragedy of the Commons" structure is to make the long-term impact on the common resource real and immediate for the individual users. To do this, determine the cost of future loss and translate it into a measurement or description that gets the players' attention.

- Another leverage point is to find the central value, vision, or management responsibility that takes the big-picture, long-term view of commons usage into account and that contains ideas for controlling allocation of the shared resource. Establishing cooperative structures or strengthening existing ones can also help. Finally, in some cases, management of the commons by a governing body can be a valid, valuable option.

To avert a "Tragedy of the Commons" dynamic, following the process described above may help, especially if done at the *outset* of an enterprise.

The critical and challenging steps will be to identify and get agreement on the commons, its limits and the real potential for its depletion, the impact of individual use on the commons, and the mechanisms required to measure and allocate usage.

In Summary

Like "Limits to Success," "Tragedy of the Commons" can help us explore the implications of finite resources. And like "Success to the Successful," this complex archetype can shed new light on the ramifications of using shared resources. "Tragedy of the Commons" steers us toward considering how to monitor usage and the limits of a common resource, and points out the need for cooperation and overall management of the resource. Similarly, this archetype can encourage us to consider the consequences of plans for growth. It highlights key assumptions about the use of resources and about the impact of growth on those resources.

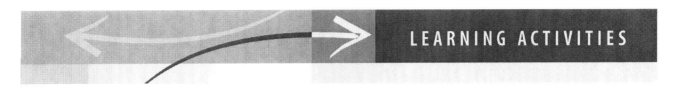

LEARNING ACTIVITIES

Now that you've learned about "Tragedy of the Commons," try your hand at the Learning Activities below. These exercises will give you an opportunity to identify a "Tragedy of the Commons" dynamic in a story, and to analyze a "Tragedy of the Commons" story from your own experience.

In each Learning Activity, you will be asked to provide:

- A statement of the theme of the story
- A list of key variables
- A graph of the key variables' distinctive behavior over time
- A causal loop diagram of the systemic structure generating the "Tragedy of the Commons" situation.

After completing the Learning Activities below, compare your responses with those in Appendix A. Don't worry if your responses look different from the ones in the appendix; there's no one right "answer" in a systems thinking analysis. These activities are mainly meant to get you thinking about the themes, patterns of behavior, and systemic structure of the archetypes.

ACTIVITY 1 THE TRAGEDY OF THE OVERBURDENED SUPPLIER

The Story ➤ State Electric & Gas is a major employer with many offices and plants. The Metropolitan division begins contracting with TempPower for security personnel, cleaning services, clerical support, and several other long- and short-term temporary workers. Managers at Metropolitan are generally very satisfied with the workers supplied by TempPower; they are trained, personable, and ready to get down to work.

Managers at the Southeast division of SE&G hear about Metropolitan's success with TempPower. So as need arises for food-service workers, drivers, guards, and other help, managers of different functions begin doing business with TempPower. Unbeknownst to State Electric & Gas, TempPower managers begin to joke about their "merger" with the utility.

One day, the managers at both the Metropolitan and Southeast divisions notice that they're experiencing some disappointment with TempPower workers. Most of the temps are high quality, but some seem unprepared or lacking in the right attitude. Then the Northeast division of SE&G sets up a contract with TempPower, and eventually everyone notices that TempPower workers just aren't what they used to be.

INSTRUCTIONS

1. Summarize the "Tragedy of the Commons" theme in this story in two or three sentences.

2. Identify the key variables in the story.

   The Metropolitan division's _____ goes up, leading to increasing

   _____, which prompts them to continue.

   Then the Southeast division's _____ begins to rise, and they experience

   increasing _____, and are encouraged to continue.

   As both divisions manage their temporary worker needs, their total _____

   increases.

   Eventually, this increase encounters _____, and _____

   begins to decline.

3. Graph what happens over time to the individual reinforcing actions, the gains produced by those actions, and to the common resource itself.

4. Fill in the blank systems archetype template on p. 123 with the variables you identified. Label each arrow in the diagram with an "s" or an "o."

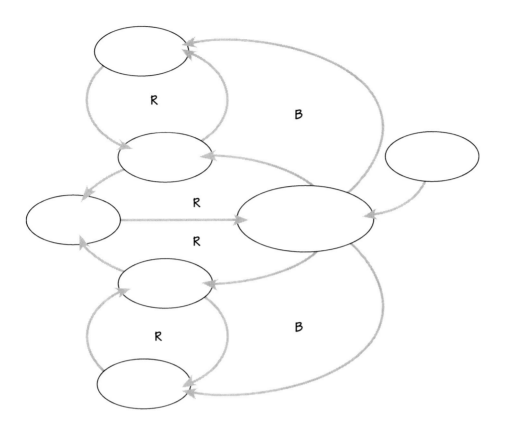

5. What can State Electric & Gas do to turn this situation around?

ACTIVITY 2   **YOUR OWN "TRAGEDY OF THE COMMONS" STORY**

INSTRUCTIONS

Follow the steps below.

STEP 1: Choose a possible "Tragedy of the Commons" situation from work, home, community, or elsewhere. Pick one that has some history so you can clearly see actual trends.

STEP 2: Make some notes about the story, enough to remind yourself of what has been happening.

STEP 3: Summarize the story in a couple of sentences. (You may find it is easier to come back to this step after you have worked with the variables and the loop diagram.)

STEP 4: List the key variables in the story.

The individual growth or success process:

The common resource:

The limit of the resource:

The impact of reaching the limit:

STEP 5: Draw the pattern of behavior over time of the variables you identified above. To confirm your graph, check with colleagues, friends, or family members to see whether your memory of the pattern of behavior matches theirs.

STEP 6: Using the "Tragedy of the Commons" causal loop template on p. 125, diagram your situation. To confirm your diagram, walk through the logic of the loops. Do you have a generic view of what's going on that all the other players would agree with? Is your mental model of the common resource clearly defined? Validate and broaden your insight further by showing your diagram to a friend, colleague, or family member. Remember to position the diagram as your "first-draft" attempt to understand what has been going on. Explain the diagram in terms of a common resource that participants in the system are depleting (knowingly or unknowingly), the motivations of the individuals involved, and the cumulative effects of the actions of many individuals. Be sure to ask what the other person thinks and whether your explanation makes sense. Don't worry if your viewpoints are different. Everyone's version of the story is a unique mental model, and the point is to learn about the role of mental models in the problems facing us.

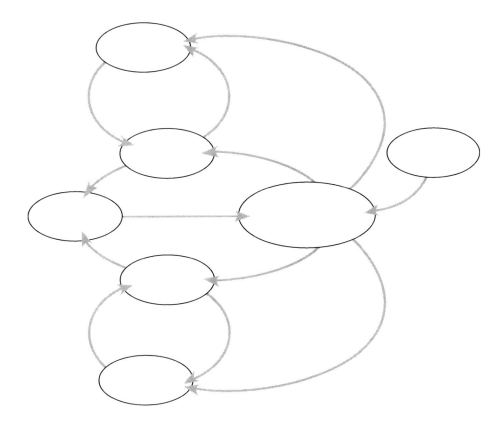

STEP 7: What ideas do you have for improving the situation in the story you chose—making the long-term impact of commons usage more concrete in the present? identifying a central management structure?

Notes

1. From "Too Many Boats on the Horizon," by Colleen Lannon, *The Systems Thinker*, Volume 5, Number 7, September 1994 (Pegasus Communications, Inc.).

2. From "'Tragedy of the Commons': All for One and None for All," *Systems Archetypes I: Designing High-Leverage Interventions*, by Daniel H. Kim (Pegasus Communications, 1992).

3. From "Using 'Tragedy of the Commons' to Link Local Action to Global Outcomes," *Systems Archetypes II: Using Systems Archetypes to Take Effective Action*, by Daniel H. Kim (Pegasus Communications, 1994).

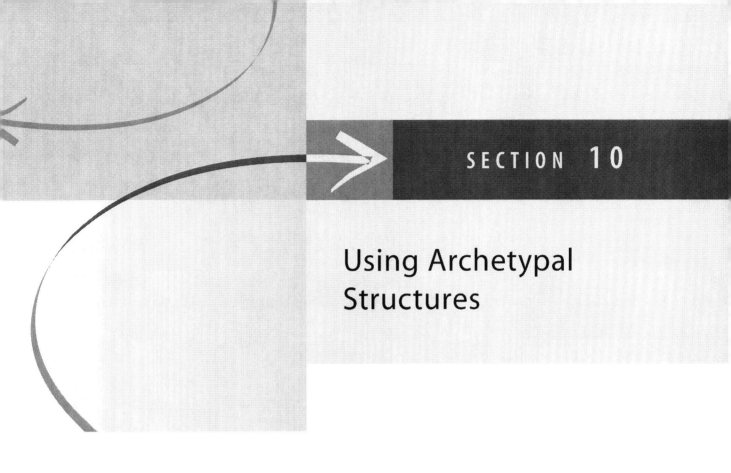

Using Archetypal Structures

So many archetypes, so many choices! How can you best use these systems thinking tools? There are many different ways to use the archetypes. Sometimes the most helpful learning experience is to start with an archetype that you suspect may be operating and create your own version of the structure by adapting your story to the archetype template. (This is what you did in all the Learning Activities in this workbook.) Other times, it can be more valuable to analyze a story without any archetype in mind at first. As you gather information about the story, you can then use a combination of tools such as behavior over time graphs and causal loop diagrams to decide whether a particular archetype may be at work in your story. Finally, you can also use the complete set of archetypes as "lenses" for looking at different aspects of problems. "Trying on" the different archetypes while addressing a problem can reveal whole new insights.

In this section, we explore these different approaches to using the archetypes and offer some examples to get you started on your way.

UNCOVERING THE LURKING ARCHETYPE

In addressing a problem, how do you know which systems archetype—if any—most applies to your situation? There are several ways to determine this:

- Listening to the theme of the story
- Examining the trends or behavior over time of certain variables in the story
- Exploring causal loop diagrams of the situation
- Using structure-behavior pairs—behavior over time graphs paired with causal loop diagrams

Listening for Storylines

As you saw in each section of this workbook, every systems archetype has its own "storyline"—a theme or direction that characterizes the behavior of the archetype's systemic structure. For example, "Escalation" tells the story of competition, rivalry, and an accelerating spiral of reactive moves. The theme of "Limits to Success" is growth, acceleration, and expansion followed by stalling out, plateauing, or decline or crash, with the suggestion that the "seeds of destruction" are somehow linked to the growth process itself.

When you hear stories in your organization, or relate your own accounts, listen for the storylines underlying the details. You may find that something in the story resonates with one of the archetypal themes. Or if you refer to the sections in this workbook, you may then recognize a storyline that echoes something in the stories you're hearing or telling.

Examining Behavior Over Time

Behavior over time graphs can help reveal systems archetypes at work because they depict the "signature" behavior patterns that each archetype typically shows. These graphs let you use past patterns to gain insight into the causal connections among variables in the story. Focusing on the pattern of observed data reduces the common temptation to force-fit a problem into a particular archetype storyline.

Let's use Custom Manufacturing, Inc., a fictional enterprise, as an example of how to work through this process.[1] CMI specializes in customizing a commodity material to meet the needs of its clients, who then produce end-products for consumers. Orders generally come in monthly, and turn-around time is about two weeks per order. CMI has successfully created a niche in a growing market and experienced steady growth over two years.

However, in the last six months, demand has fluctuated wildly. At first, managers assumed that this trend signaled turbulence in the marketplace because of new entrants in the specialty materials niche. The managers naturally want to remain competitive, and decided that a deeper understanding of the systemic structure driving these fluctuations would help

FIGURE 10.1

Demand at CMI

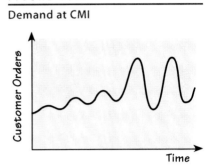

FIGURE 10.2

CMI's Causal Loop Diagram

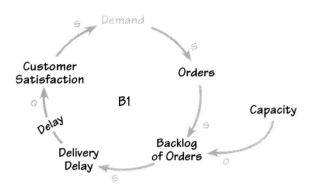

them stabilize the company's order stream. They did not want just to react to market trends, but to learn to work *with* the system.

They began by graphing demand over the last two years (see Figure 10.1, "Demand at CMI"). The graph showed a clearly oscillating pattern that had worsened in the last six months—a possible clue that a particular archetype was at work. Because the oscillation especially suggested a balancing process with delays, the managers gathered data and talked to customers to find out what might have caused the changes in demand. Drawing the BOT graph helped CMI take its first step in identifying what was going on.

Exploring Causal Loop Diagrams

After drawing a behavior over time graph, it can be helpful to then build a causal loop diagram and look for similarities to the archetypal structures. There are certain combinations of loops that hint at particular archetypes, but you should always check your assumptions—especially about behavior over time—against the storyline. Not all combinations of loops constitute an archetypal structure. Many causal loop diagrams contain several balancing and reinforcing loops linked together without necessarily matching a particular archetypal storyline.

Let's see how CMI employed this strategy in addressing their fluctuating demand. Using all the information they gathered from their BOT graph and from their discussions with customers, CMI's managers then created a causal loop diagram that told the following story (see Figure 10.2, "CMI's Causal Loop Diagram"): As demand increases, the number of orders to be processed increases. Processing customized orders requires specially trained machinists, so when demand exceeds staff capacity, backlog grows and delivery delays lengthen. But CMI's customers have their own stream of customer orders to fill. So when CMI's delivery time extends beyond an acceptable limit (usually three weeks), customers get dissatisfied and go to the higher priced competitors, and orders at CMI gradually decline.

Each time the backlog reached a critical level, CMI's managers added temporary staff, which, combined with the decrease in incoming orders, brought down the backlog and shortened delivery times. However, it took several weeks for regular customers to learn of improved delivery times and then shift orders back to CMI. Thus, the demand for products oscillated as a function of the company's internal capacity to respond to orders. To CMI, this diagram looked suspiciously like the heart of a "Growth and Underinvestment" process, and the company began considering ways to manage the dynamic.

CMI had previously assumed that periodic downturns in orders resulted from competitive pressures or cyclical trends in the market. This systemic analysis suggested that their internal policies could be making the situation worse. Therefore, managers instituted a flexible workforce policy and cross-trained machinists. These steps helped them staff up immediately with experienced people when the need arose, rather than hiring temporary staff during backlog times and suffering the effects of the delay between the temps' arrival and their effectiveness in reducing the backlog.

Using Structure-Behavior Pairs

When a behavior over time graph is paired with its corresponding causal loop structure, the resulting "structure-behavior pair" can also provide a clue as to certain archetypes at work (see "Structure-Behavior Pairs"). As you saw in sections 2–9, each archetype has its own distinctive BOT pattern and structural template.

As you sketch your own BOT graphs and CLDs, look for resemblances to one or more of the systems archetype structure-behavior pairs. Finding a match can open up new approaches to your problem and get you thinking about the ramifications the match may have for your particular situation.

APPLYING THE ARCHETYPES[2]

When you use the archetypes to gain insight into a situation or problem, you may find it helpful to start with a specific archetype and work "backwards." That is, the archetypes themselves can provide starting points for your exploration. Note that applying archetypes to a specific problem in this way can be confusing or difficult if you believe there is only one right way to use them. There are actually several different strategies for applying the archetypes: using them as different "lenses," as structural pattern templates, and as dynamic theories.

Seeing Through an Archetype "Lens"

Many of us have said, "I'll believe it when I see it," suggesting that we have faith primarily in what we can see and touch. If there are 100 cases of beer in inventory, and you and your coworker both count them, you can both agree on the number. However, if someone asks *why* there are

STRUCTURE-BEHAVIOR PAIRS

Behavior	Structure	Description

Exponential Growth/Decay

Exponential growth or decay usually indicates the presence of a reinforcing process.

Growing Action — R — Condition or Performance (s, s)

Time

Goal-Seeking Behavior

Goal-seeking behavior is characterized by a simple balancing process, which seeks to close the gap between a goal (whether implicit or explicit) and the actual condition.

Goal

Desired Level — Gap (o) — Corrective Action (s) — Actual Level (s) — B

Time

Oscillation

An oscillation is caused by a balancing process with significant delays, which creates under- and over-adjustment around the goal.

Desired Level — Gap (o) — Delay — Corrective Action (s) — Delay — Actual Level (s) — B

Time

S-Shaped Growth

S-shaped growth is the result of a reinforcing process that has become "stalled" by a balancing process.

Constraint

Efforts — R — Performance — B — Limiting Action (s, s, s, o)

Time

100 cases in inventory, your opinions are likely to be different and colored by your personal beliefs and mental models. One of you may think the 100 cases are in inventory as a result of poor production scheduling, and you will find evidence to support that view. The other person may think that individual error is responsible for overstocking, and therefore focuses on finding someone to blame rather than looking for the systemic forces behind the problem. We don't believe what we see as often as we see what we believe. Because it is easy to fall into this trap, systems thinking tools such as the archetypes help us stay focused on the broader systemic issues.

In many ways, using an archetype is like putting on a special pair of eyeglasses. If you look at a situation through the lens of "Shifting the Burden," you ask different questions and focus on different elements than if you had used "Tragedy of the Commons" as a lens. It is not so much a question of which archetype is "right," but rather what insights each archetype offers.

Using the archetypes as lenses requires a basic understanding of the main lessons, key elements, and outcomes or high-leverage actions that each one embodies. This level of understanding lets you go into a situation, identify potential themes, explore their implications, and gain a better understanding of the problem. The key question is not, "Is this 'Shifting the Burden' or 'Fixes That Fail'?" but "Is it helpful to view this particular situation as a 'Shifting the Burden'? What can we learn, and what insights can we gain, by doing so? On the other hand, what could we learn if we viewed the situation as a 'Fixes That Fail'?"

Overfishing and "Tragedy of the Commons."

For example, let's consider the problem of fish depletion in coastal waters. In order to address the dangers of overfishing and eventual depletion of certain species, the U.S. government launched a program to buy boats back from fishermen.

The overfishing problem has all the classic features of a "Tragedy of the Commons" archetype. A large number of players are exploiting a single resource, and the incentive is for each fisherman to catch as many fish as possible. However, the total of the fishermen's efforts eventually hurts everyone as fish stocks become depleted. The irony of the situation is that, despite the devastation in the long term, it is in no individual's economic interest to stop fishing in the short term. In addition, most fishermen probably love their life on the sea and care about the fate of the fish; they would be hard pressed to give up their livelihood.

Where is the leverage in this structure? One possibility that often arises in a "Tragedy of the Commons" is to have a single governing authority manage the "commons." From this perspective, the boat buyback program can be seen as an appropriate role for the government as resource manager.

Overfishing and "Shifting the Burden."

If you look at the same situation through the lens of another archetype, however, you see some different, potentially relevant issues. For example, "Shifting the Burden" is about a problem symptom that cries out to be

TRYING ON DIFFERENT "EYEGLASSES"

Systems Archetypes	Questions to Ask
Fixes That Fail	• Have actions been taken to respond quickly to a crisis without much consideration of long-term consequences? • Have similar actions been taken in the past in response to similar crises?
Shifting the Burden	• Are actions taken to alleviate problem symptoms shifting attention away from more fundamental solutions? • Are there additional consequences that systematically erode the underlying capability of the organization?
Limits to Success	• Are once-successful programs experiencing diminishing returns? • Are there limits in the system that are constraining the growth?
Drifting Goals	• Are there goals or standards that are eroding over time? • Are people focused on achieving the goal or on reducing the discomfort of not being at the goal? • Are some goals being met at the expense of others?
Growth and Underinvestment	• Do investments tend to be made as a reaction to growth rather than in anticipation of growth? • Do problems created by growth, rather than long-range planning, act as the organizational signal to invest? • What would happen if investments were made earlier, in anticipation of limits to growth?
Success to the Successful	• Is there a resource for which allocation decisions are in a zero-sum game? • Does the success of each party depend on receiving the same resource? • Does allocation of the fixed resource depend on success of the parties involved?
Escalation	• Are there two or more players whose individual actions can be perceived as a threat by the others? • Does each player have the capacity to respond to a sense of threat with actions similar to the other party's?
Tragedy of the Commons	• Is there a large number of players who have free or equal access to a common and limited resource? • Is the system set up to be self-regulated, with no overarching governing body? • Is there any regulatory or coordinating mechanism for managing the commons? If so, is it effective?

fixed. In such situations, there is a tendency to implement a solution that alleviates the symptom in the short term rather than to invest in a more lasting solution. Implementing the quick fix reduces the pressure to examine the deeper structures that may be at the root of the problem.

From the "Shifting the Burden" point of view, we might be concerned that the government bail-out will send the signal that Uncle Sam will provide a safety net whenever the fishing industry develops overcapacity. Therefore, when fishing stocks replenish, fishermen may be less careful about taking risks and expanding their fleets. Over time, the buyback program may become so entrenched that it turns into a permanent quick fix that shifts the wrong kind of responsibility to the government. In this case, "Shifting the Burden" reveals how the short-term solution shifts the burden of risk and overextension from the individual to the government.

The buyback example illustrates how the archetypes can be used to gain different perspectives on an issue. Rather than spending a lot of time figuring out which archetype best matches your particular situation or struggling to diagram a situation "correctly," you can use the archetypes to initiate a broader inquiry into the problem.

To see which lenses may be relevant and what insights each archetype adds to your problem, use the questions listed in "Trying on Different 'Eyeglasses'" on p. 133. Once you have selected the most pertinent archetype(s), refer to the appropriate sections in this workbook for guidelines on developing action plans to address the problem systemically.

Looking at the world through the lenses of archetypes puts your primary focus on systemic structures and not on individuals or particular events. This refocusing is particularly important at the initial stage of problem diagnosis because it lets you engage people in the inquiry process without triggering defensiveness. The process of trying on different "lenses" will lead you to ask different kinds of questions and ultimately help you have more productive conversations.

Using Archetypes as Structural Pattern Templates

In addition to resembling "lenses" for addressing issues, archetypes can serve as structural pattern templates. An archetype serves in this way when it helps you "see" a problem at the structural level—at the level of interrelated variables—rather than at the level of linear, cause-and-effect detail. With this structural-level perspective, you focus more on relationships and pay attention to larger "chunks" of the system (see "Archetypes as Structural Pattern Templates"). Furthermore, as you develop familiarity with a repertoire of structural patterns or archetypes, you start seeing how today's issue might be similar to last month's issue, and you can apply what you learned earlier to new situations. It's actually very effective to approach a new problem by comparing it to another problem that you've already solved. Honing our proficiency with the systems archetypes increases our personal inventory of solved problems, examples, and stories that all give us insights into new problems that may come along.

Loop Combinations and Archetypes.

As you saw in the CMI story, sometimes a particular combination of causal loops can suggest a certain archetype. Below are some guidelines

ARCHETYPES AS STRUCTURAL PATTERN TEMPLATES

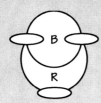

FIXES THAT FAIL

Efforts to bring something into balance create consequences that reinforce the need to take more action.

SHIFTING THE BURDEN

Two balancing loops compete for control in "solving" a problem symptom, while a reinforcing side-effect of one solution makes the problem worse.

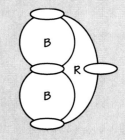

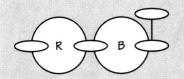

LIMITS TO SUCCESS

A reinforcing loop creates pressure in the system that is relieved by one or more balancing loops tha slow growth.

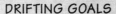

DRIFTING GOALS

Two balancing loops strive to close the gap between a goal and current reality.

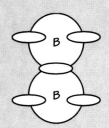

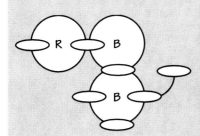

GROWTH AND UNDERINVESTMENT

A "Limits to Success" structure has a specific system constraint—namely, an investment-policy balancing loop.

SUCCESS TO THE SUCCESSFUL

Two reinforcing loops compete for a common, limited resource.

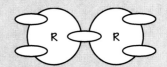

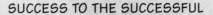

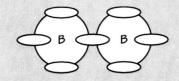

ESCALATION

Two or more players manage their own balancing loop in response to the threatening actions of others.

TRAGEDY OF THE COMMONS

The sum total of two or more reinforcing activities strains a limited resource and creates balancing consequences for all.

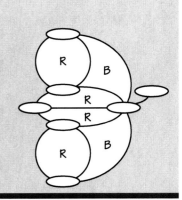

for using these special loop combinations. As you review these guidelines, it's important to remember that the archetypes are not "out there" in the world. They are models of systemic structures, and therefore exist only in our heads. The advantage to them is that we can use them as templates through which to view the world.

- *Balancing process followed by reinforcing process:* This combination often signals a "Fixes That Fail" situation. Check for a second balancing process to see whether "Shifting the Burden" is also at work. In essence, "Shifting the Burden" is a more complex version of "Fixes That Fail."

- *A pair of balancing processes:* This combination is the most open-ended and occurs in many archetypes. A pair of balancing loops could be the core of a "Shifting the Burden" situation. To verify, check especially for quick fixes and fundamental solutions. It could also be "Escalation." To verify, look for the competitive, reactive spiral. Two balancing loops also occur in "Drifting Goals" as well; to identify this situation, see whether a goal and a gap exist. In addition, this pair of loops could be part of "Growth and Underinvestment." Check for an associated reinforcing loop and listen for the investment element of the story. Finally, the more complex archetypes, such as "Tragedy of the Commons," also contain paired balancing loops; look for the identifying themes to verify.

- *A reinforcing process followed by a balancing process:* This combination is the essence of "Limits to Success" as well as the first phase of "Growth and Underinvestment." The combination can also be found in the more complex archetypes; to determine, pay especially close attention to the storyline.

- *A pair of reinforcing processes:* If the trend or the story theme emphasizes the growth of one entity in parallel to the deterioration of another, then this combination signals "Success to the Successful." Otherwise, the reinforcing processes might be components of one of the more complex archetypes, depending on the storyline.

Using Archetypes as Dynamic Theories

In order to make sense of our experience of the world, we must be able to relate that experience to a coherenet, explanatory story. In other words, we need to create a theory about what we *don't* know based on something we *do* know. Each systems archetype embodies a particular theory about dynamic behavior that can serve as a starting point for selecting and formulating raw data into a coherent, explicit set of causal relationships (see the brief summaries of these theories in "Archetypes as Dynamic Theories"). Then, the archetypes can guide us further in testing those relationships through direct observation, data analysis, or group deliberation.

In addition, each archetype offers prescriptions for effective action. When we recognize an archetype at work, we can use the theory behind it to explore the problem and work toward an intervention. For example, if you're looking at a potential "Fixes That Fail" situation, the theory of

ARCHETYPES AS DYNAMIC THEORIES

Systems Archetypes	Theory
Fixes That Fail	A "quick-fix" solution can have unintended consequences that worsen the original problem.
Shifting the Burden	When a symptomatic solution is applied to a problem symptom, it alleviates the symptom, reduces pressure to implement a fundamental solution, and has a side-effect that undermines the ability to develop a fundamental solution.
Limits to Success	A reinforcing process of growth or expansion will encounter a balancing process as the limit of the system is approached.
Drifting Goals	When a gap exists between a goal and reality, the goal is often lowered to close the gap. Eventually, the lowering of the goal leads to deteriorating performance.
Growth and Underinvestment	When growth approaches a limit, the system compensates by lowering performance standards. This reduces perceived need for capacity investments and leads to lower performance, justifying further underinvestment.
Success to the Successful	In a system with limited resources, one party's initial success justifies devoting more resources to that party, which widens the performance gap between the various parties.
Escalation	A perception of threat causes one party to take actions that are then perceived as threatening by another party. The parties keep trying to outdo one another in a reinforcing spiral of competition.
Tragedy of the Commons	If total usage of a common resource grows too great, the commons will become overloaded or depleted, and everyone will experience diminishing benefits.

that archetype suggests that a "quick-fix" solution can have unintended consequences that ultimately worsen the original problem. Your awareness of this theory can help you keep an eye out for solutions that look promising but that may be quick fixes in disguise. The "Fixes That Fail" archetype theory also encourages you to think about the possible long-term ramifications of your decisions and actions.

By using the theory behind each archetype as a springboard for exploration, you can develop insights about how best to approach a problem, and can prepare for and address long-range developments.

Congratulations on completing *Systems Archetype Basics: From Story to Structure!* With your new knowledge of this powerful class of systems thinking tools, you're ready to go out and start using the archetypes to enrich your own life. Keep an eye out for opportunities to practice using the archetypes as much as possible. But remember this key lesson as you do so: The archetypes are especially valuable for generating new and expansive questions in response to problems you encounter and stories you hear. For example, "What unintended long-term effects might that solution have?" "What pressure will we relieve with this response to the problem?" "Is there something we don't do now to solve the problem because it's too expensive or time consuming?" "What aspect of our organization might slow down or stop this planned growth strategy?"

There's another important lesson to remember from this workbook: Not every story fits perfectly into one of the archetypes. As you begin applying the archetypes to situations in your own life, resist the temptation to force-fit stories into the archetypes. Instead, use the archetypes to open up new insights and perspectives, and try to see them as a beginning rather than an end to your investigations.

Finally, explore various uses of the archetypes *with others as much as possible.* These tools are particularly beneficial when used in a group effort. Sharing ideas, insights, and perspectives will lead you to much richer learning experiences than if you were to work with the archetypes alone.

As we discussed at the beginning of this workbook, people in all cultures have encapsulated the most important and meaningful of life's lessons in their stories and epics. In their own way, the archetypes serve the same function for "students" of organizational learning. *Listen* for the archetypal stories. *Watch* for the hints and signals that a familiar dynamic is at work. Then *tell* the stories and *help* your colleagues explore the meaning of the stories with you. Let each listener contribute his or her understanding of the story. *Then let the questions and exploration begin!*

Notes

1. This story is adapted from "Structure-Behavior Pairs: A Starting Point for Problem Diagnosis," by Colleen Lannon, *The Systems Thinker,* Volume 7, Number 6, August 1996 (Pegasus Communications, Inc.).

2. From *Applying Systems Archetypes,* by Daniel H. Kim and Colleen Lannon, *Innovations in Management Series* (Pegasus Communications, 1997).

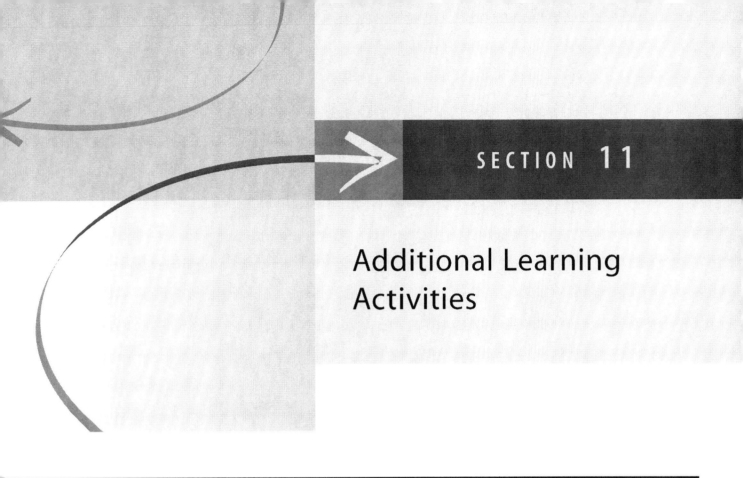

Additional Learning Activities

Now that you've learned about the archetypes and considered some of the ways to apply them, here are some additional opportunities to practice. Each of these cases involves at least one archetype. In some of them, more than one archetype are at work. For example, you know that a "Fixes That Fail" situation can also be examined from the "Shifting the Burden" perspective to understand how addressing a problem symptom prevents a more enduring solution from taking hold.

In other cases, you may see one archetypal structure currently at work, with other archetypes possibly coming into play in the future. For example, in a "Success to the Successful" structure, the entity that is favored can also be at risk of hitting a limit and falling into a "Limits to Success" dynamic. Other growth situations are at risk of becoming "Tragedy of the Commons."

LEARNING ACTIVITIES

In each of the learning activities below, you'll be asked to provide:

- A brief summary of a story's theme and the underlying archetype(s)
- A list of key variables in the story
- A graph of the behavior over time of the key variables from the story
- A causal loop diagram
- An analysis of additional archetypes that might be at work
- A prediction of archetypal structures that the story may evolve into.

Activity 1   REFORMING SCHOOLS[1]

The Story ➤ These days, many education-reform proposals call for various changes in the system, such as more financial investment, different curricula, or longer school days. Some programs suggest allowing parents to choose schools, and through a voucher system, letting market forces determine quality. Still other reform advocates believe that schools should simply go back to teaching the basics. A common assumption behind each of these proposals is that the basic design of the educational system is sound—it just needs some changes.

As a result of this assumption, most attempts to fix the educational system focus on trying to improve the individual parts of the system. The overall approach is to fix the broken pieces. But because the causes of the current education crisis are so complex and deeply embedded, only fundamental changes in the structure of the system will have lasting results. Lengthening the school day won't help if students are not learning during the time they already spend in the classroom. Testing teachers won't improve their skills if they were not well trained in the first place. Tightening standards and testing students will not make any difference if the standards are irrelevant to today's needs. There must be a profound shift in thinking and inquiry into the nature of change in education; otherwise, reform efforts might actually make things worse. As just one example, attempts to "fix" low test scores may involve setting up focused classes on exam-taking techniques, which can improve scores. This focus, however, could reinforce the belief among students that education is about "performing," and more fundamental ways to engage students' interest in learning will be lost.

INSTRUCTIONS

1. Briefly summarize the point of the story. What theme do you notice? What archetype do you think is at work?

2. Identify the key variables in the example about test scores at the end of the story.

3. Graph the behavior over time of those variables.

4. Using the variables, create a causal loop diagram. If you discover an additional variable, include it in your diagram and add it to the list of variables. When you complete the diagram, walk through it with the story to make sure it depicts the dynamics. Also check the diagram against your BOT graph to ensure that it captures the changes that occur over time.

5. Looking at the diagram, what archetype do you see?

6. What other archetypes might be involved in this situation?

7. Are there any other archetypes that might come into play in the future?

8. What are the management or intervention guidelines suggested by the archetypes you identified?

ACTIVITY 2   CUSTOMER SERVICE DILEMMAS[2]

The Story ➤ UpDate News, a city newspaper, has begun to notice that advertiser service levels are oscillating. During some publication periods, ads are ready on time, with no changes, and the copy is accurate. With other publication periods, however, performance goes through the floor: Everything's late, some items miss deadlines completely, swarms of changes are requested, and hundreds of mistakes crop up. When the editors check with the advertising service staff, they discover that the staff is experiencing cycles of tremendous time pressure. When they look into advertiser sales, they see a steady rise in sales, but also discover reports of irregular advertiser satisfaction.

In the advertising service department, when sales increase, there are more advertisers sending in more ad copy and calling in with more requests and changes. The same number of people have to respond to more calls, orders, and requests—and still meet the same print deadlines. The staff's first reaction is always to work harder, put in more effort, skip breaks and meals, and thereby increase their productivity. For a while, more work does get done. However, if the crunch persists, morale might eventually drop and hurt productivity.

Ultimately, when the time pressure gets too great, quality could also decline (inaccurate copy, missing ads). After a while, rising dissatisfaction might discourage advertisers from buying ad space. The decline in demand, however, would take some of the pressure out of the system, providing relief to the service department.

INSTRUCTIONS

1. Briefly summarize the theme(s) you notice in the story. What archetype or archetypes do you think is or are at work?

2. Identify the key variables from the story. You may find that two or more variables may be aggregated into a single higher-level variable.

3. Graph the behavior over time of those variables.

4. Using the variables, create a causal loop diagram. If you discover an additional variable, include it in your diagram and add it to the list of variables. When you complete the diagram, walk through it with the story to make sure it depicts the dynamics. Also check it against your BOT graph to ensure that it captures the changes that occur over time.

5. Looking at the diagram, what archetypes do you notice?

6. Are there any other archetypes that might come into play in the future?

7. What are the management or intervention guidelines suggested by the archetypes you identified?

ACTIVITY 3   **BALANCING WORK AND FAMILY**[3]

The Story ➤ Each of us has a certain amount of time and attention to give to the priorities in our lives. The more time we devote to work, the more successful we may become, which fuels our desire to put more time into work. A similar result may occur if we devote our time and energy to family or to community work or to sports and fitness. Most of us struggle to maintain a balance between two or more major priorities in our lives.

Suppose, however, that a high-priority project forces you to put in longer hours at work for an extended period of time. The time away from your other priorities—let's say your family in this case—begins to create tensions at home. Your spouse complains that you are never at home. Your children are upset about your not coming to their school events. Your parents comment that you don't call or come by much these days.

When you do have time at home, you get hit with the accumulated chores—the garden, the closets, last season's gear to be stored. Plus, there's the pent-up demand for your attention— conversations, decisions, social events, school obligations, and unresolved arguments, adolescent crises, hurt feelings. All in all, home suddenly seems like an unpleasant, high-pressure place to be. So, you withdraw further from the family, devoting yourself even more to your project at the office.

Your work on the project is starting to generate interest throughout the organization; upper managers are taking notice of your success. At the same time that praise and possibilities build up at work, complaints and tensions pile up at home.

INSTRUCTIONS

1. Briefly summarize the theme(s) in the story. What archetype(s) do you think might be at work?

2. Identify the key variables from the story. You may find that two or more variables may be aggregated into a single higher-level variable.

3. Graph the behavior over time of those variables.

4. Using the variables, create a causal loop diagram. If you discover an additional variable, include it in your diagram and add it to the list of variables. When you complete the diagram, walk through it with the story to make sure it depicts the dynamics. Also check it against your BOT graph to ensure that it captures the changes that occur over time.

5. Looking at the diagram, what archetypes do you notice?

6. Are there any other archetypes that might come into play in the future?

7. What are the management or intervention guidelines suggested by the archetypes you identified?

ACTIVITY 4   **GETTING WHAT YOU MEASURE**[4]

The Story ➤ At ReadyMade, an international manufacturing company, the organizational development (OD) group has been noticing a couple of disturbing patterns while studying the problem-solving effectiveness of central staff employees. The OD group has already observed that, although the mission of corporate staff is to provide high-value services on a global scale, they actually spend most of their time at headquarters or in the plant across the street. In addition, OD has noticed that, while individual groups have reported that they usually receive prompt support in handling specific local problems, they often find themselves recalling their central staff consultant quite regularly. Even the internal OD consultants sometimes joke about the increasing frequency of "SWAT-team" missions to sweep up after other central staff people's "quick fixes."

But OD has uncovered another pattern as well: The better managers become at proposing and implementing quick fixes, the more likely they are to receive all of their requested budget allocations. Success at pulling in budget money encourages managers to favor the same indicators favored by senior executives—the indicators that let them select and implement quick fixes that tend to calm the waves and keep the boat from rocking.

The better that everyone gets at paying attention to the favored indicators, the more promptly problem symptoms are detected and handled. Quick fixes have proliferated. Because they're so busy and useful, central staff tends not to complain about the increasing amount of patching up they do. Just occasionally, an external consultant comments that it seems like no one ever does an in-depth analysis of the problem symptoms or of the value of the favored indicators. Consultants also suggest the possibility of replacing crisis management with proactivity. But whenever this idea pops up, people just shake their heads again about the impatience of top executives, and the meeting focuses once more on the current problem.

INSTRUCTIONS

1. Briefly summarize the theme(s) in the story. What archetype(s) do you think might be at work?

2. Identify the key variables from the story. You may find that two or more variables may be aggregated into a single higher-level variable.

3. Graph the behavior over time of those variables.

4. Using the variables, create a causal loop diagram. If you discover an additional variable, include it in your diagram and add it to the list of variables. When you complete the diagram, walk through it with the story to make sure it depicts the dynamics. Also check it against your BOT graph to ensure that it captures the changes that occur over time.

5. Looking at the diagram, what archetypes do you notice?

6. Are there any other archetypes that might come into play in the future?

7. What are the management or intervention guidelines suggested by the archetypes you identified?

Activity 5   **SURVIVING COMPETITION**[5]

The Story ➤ Parker Roberts, an electronic products company, has built its business on the premise that its products cost about the same as the market leader's, but that they either perform better or offer extra features. A succession of brilliant product development choices and engineering breakthroughs has led to high performance-to-price ratios, which have pumped up sales. Revenues are flowing into product development, and Parker Roberts is on a roll.

One day, the company notices a new pattern: As competitors' prices have decreased and product performance has improved, Parker Roberts' relative performance-to-price has come down. Sales are suffering and revenue growth has slowed. In response, Parker Roberts' financial management recommends using more parts from outside suppliers to keep prices down. The theory is that lower costs will improve margins and net income, which will ease off financial pressures. Marketing points out the risk that a reliance on outside manufacturing could degrade the premium brand image and hurt sales, which could hurt net income over the long run.

Operations suggests that the way to handle increased financial pressure is to grow sales by lowering prices—a move that might help Parker Roberts' price-performance ratio to improve immediately. In theory, subsequent growth in sales would also improve net income. Of course, lower prices also mean lower margins.

Finally, the sales organization suggests using multiple distribution channels to increase sales, by making Parker Roberts products available to a wider audience. Marketing protests that this move could also hurt the premium brand image and actually reduce sales revenues.

INSTRUCTIONS

1. Briefly summarize the theme(s) in the story. What archetype(s) do you think might be at work?

2. Identify the key variables from the story. You may find that two or more variables may be aggregated into a single higher-level variable.

3. Graph the behavior over time of those variables.

4. Using the variables, create a causal loop diagram. If you discover an additional variable, include it in your diagram and add it to the list of variables. (Note: This is a complex story. You might find it easiest to diagram "episodes" of the story, one at a time, and then link them up.) When you complete the diagram, walk through it with the story to make sure it depicts the dynamics. Also check it against your BOT graph to ensure that it captures the changes that occur over time.

5. Looking at the diagram, what archetypes do you notice?

6. Are there any other archetypes that might come into play in the future?

7. What are the management or intervention guidelines suggested by the archetypes you identified?

Notes

1. From "Redesigning Our Schools, Reinventing the Future," by Kellie Wardman O'Reilly and Daniel H. Kim, *The Systems Thinker,* Volume 3, Number 9, November 1992 (Pegasus Communications, Inc.).

2. From "Management Flight Simulators: Flight Training for Managers," by Daniel H. Kim, *The Systems Thinker,* Volume 3, Number 9, November 1992 (Pegasus Communications, Inc.).

3. From "'Success to the Successful': Self-Fulfilling Prophecies," by Daniel H. Kim, *The Systems Thinker,* Volume 3, Number 2, March 1992 (Pegasus Communications, Inc.).

4. From "A Call to Action: Designing the Future at Ford," by Vic Leo, *The Systems Thinker,* Volume 4, Number 5, June/July 1993 (Pegasus Communications, Inc.).

5. From "Charting Compaq's Future," *The Systems Thinker,* Volume 3, Number 1, February 1992 (Pegasus Communications, Inc.)

Potential Responses to the Learning Activities

SECTION 2: FIXES THAT FAIL

ACTIVITY 1   THE DANGERS OF DOWNSIZING

1. *Summarize the "Fixes That Fail" theme in this story in two or three sentences.*

   Falling profits lead the company to institute layoffs to improve profits. Layoffs have an immediate impact in improving the bottom line by cutting staff costs. Over the longer term, however, they also reduce the company's ability to respond to customers, which hurts service quality and sales. The delayed consequences of the layoffs come back full circle and lead to a further decline in profits, thereby increasing pressure to implement another quick fix.

2. *Identify the key variables in the story.*

   The problem symptom is **profits** are falling.

   The quick fix is to institute or continue **layoffs,** thus reducing [**administrative and service staff.**]

   The theory is that the quick fix will bring down **personnel costs.**

   In actuality, the quick fix also reduces [**ability to respond to customers**], which brings down **service quality** and [**perceived quality**].

   Sales fall, which worsens the problem symptom.

3. *Graph the behavior over time of the problem symptom, and show the effect of the quick fix on the graph.*

   Notice the downward trend of profits punctuated by the first two layoffs, which temporarily bring profits back up.

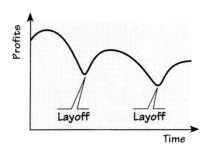

4. *Using the blank systems archetype template provided, fill in the diagram with the story's key variables.*

   Your causal loop diagram may be relatively simple, with three variables in the quick-fix loop and two more in the unintended-consequences loop. On the other hand, to see the story clearly, you may have included more variables in either or both loops.

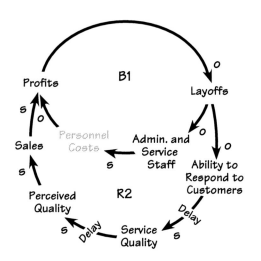

What is most important is that your loops include *at least* the variables profits, layoffs, sales, and service quality. Remember, as you deepen your understanding of a system, you can aggregate variables to simplify the diagram.

ACTIVITY 2

THE PROBLEM WITH PROMOTIONS

1. *Summarize the "Fixes That Fail" theme in this story in two or three sentences.*

Revenue pressures are increasing, so the company runs more marketing promotions intended to boost sales and reduce pressure. Over time, the promotions reduce customers' perception of the quality of the products, they turn to other companies, sales fall, and revenue pressure rises again. Actions taken to relieve revenue pressure ultimately result in increasing revenue pressure.

2. *Identify the key variables in the story.*

Problem symptom: **Revenue pressure**

Quick fix: **Promotions**

Quick-fix result that will relieve the problem symptom: **Increased sales**

Unintended consequence of the quick fix (name one or two): **Negative perception of quality** and **Declining sales**.

3. *Graph the behavior of the problem symptom and the effect of the quick fix.*

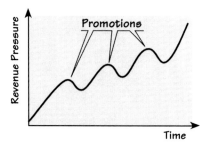

4. *Using the blank systems archetype template, fill in the diagram with the variables you identified.*

Notice that this causal loop diagram looks a little different from the previous one. The unintended-consequences loop links up with the quick-fix loop at "Sales" instead of at the problem symptom of revenue pressure. As you become more experienced, you will find that what is most important about mapping an archetype is capturing the essential set of loop relationships, not trying to fit the diagram into one particular form. The essential relationship in "Fixes That Fail" is how a balancing loop action causes a reinforcing loop action that makes the original problem symptom worse.

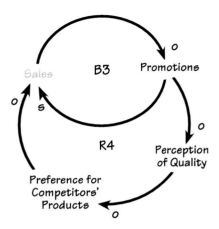

ACTIVITY 3   CAR LEASES THAT FAIL

1. *Summarize the "Fixes That Fail" theme in this story in two or three sentences.*

   In an attempt to maintain profits, auto makers offer aggressive leasing deals that do encourage sales, bring in more revenue, and boost profits. As leases become more aggressive, the accuracy of actual residuals or market value declines and auto makers take losses on more deals, which hurt profits.

2. *Identify the key variables in the story.*

   Problem symptom: **Stagnant or declining profits** [increasing pressure to maintain profits]

   Quick fix: **Aggressive leases** [more competitive, more cut-rate leases]

   Quick-fix results that will relieve the problem symptom: **Increased unit sales** and **increased revenue** [car sales, leasing revenue]

   Unintended consequence(s) of quick fix: Decline in **accuracy of actual residuals**, and **financial losses from residuals;** [residual values; accuracy of market value; financial return]

3. *Graph the behavior of the problem symptom and the effect of the quick fix.*

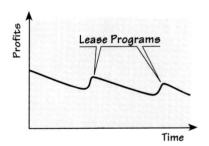

4. *Using the blank systems archetype template, fill in the diagram with the variables you identified.*

   Increasingly aggressive leases, including high residuals, do not automatically mean that the overall accuracy of actual market values (actual residuals) will go down. However, in an industry that is notorious for hyperbole and an immediate-term focus, the risk of inaccurate market predictions is always present. If you were using the "Fixes That Fail" archetype to examine potential unintended consequences of an aggressive leasing campaign, the accuracy issue is one dynamic you would do well to explore.

Note that we can simplify the above diagram by collapsing some of the variables in loop R6, as shown below.

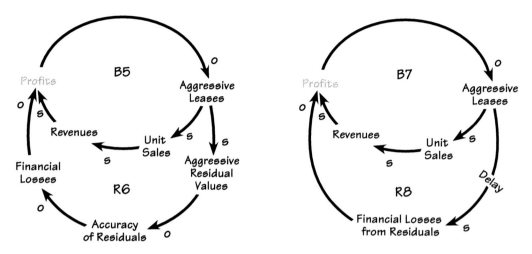

SECTION 3: SHIFTING THE BURDEN

ACTIVITY 1   **PRICE PROMOTIONS: WHAT ARE THEY REALLY PUSHING?**

1. *Summarize the "Shifting the Burden" theme in this story in two or three sentences.*

   As product sales drop, manufacturers respond to pressure by increasing the number of price promotions. A more fundamental solution to the problem could be to invest in improvements in brand image and quality. However, the increasing use of price promotions has "hooked" retailers on the subsidies they receive, which in turn reduce manufacturers' funds available to invest in brand image and quality.

2. *Identify the key variables in the story.*

   The problem symptom is that **sales** are falling.

   The quick fix is to institute or continue **price promotions.**

   A more fundamental solution is to invest in **improvements to brand image and quality**.

   The quick fix also increases **subsidies to retailers,** which cut into **funds available for investment [in brand image and quality]**, and thus undermine the manufacturers' ability to support the more fundamental solution.

3. *Graph the behavior over time of the symptomatic solution and the fundamental solution.*

   Your graph might show a simple "X" shape, with increasing use of price promotions and decreasing funds for investment in brand image and quality. The X might also have wavering "legs" representing the intermittent effectiveness of the quick fix alternating with its loss of effectiveness.

   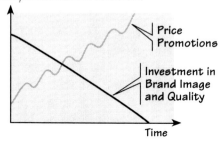

4. *Fill in the blank systems archetype template with the variables you identified. Feel free to add extra variables to any loop in the template. Be sure to label each arrow in your diagram with an "s" or an "o," to show "same" or "opposite" change, and show any important delays.*

The fundamental solution loop might contain "improvements in brand image and quality," or "investments in brand image and quality." Both are accurate. This example is a variation of the one encountered in Activity 2 of "Fixes That Fail." With "Shifting the Burden," we take a deeper look into the issue by working to identify what we believe to be a more fundamental solution than the quick fix. To see the "Fixes That Fail" structure, you can add the reinforcing loop between Price Promotions and Consumer Goods Sales.

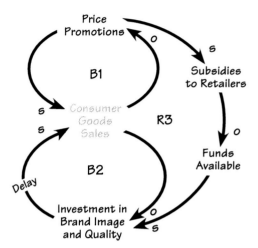

ACTIVITY 2 **ADDICTION TO BLAME**

1. *Summarize the "Shifting the Burden" theme in this story in two or three sentences.*

When errors occur and stress goes up, people at ABCo tend to blame someone. The result is that willingness to share information and communicate freely has been reduced or has disappeared. A more fundamental solution is to develop methods and processes to clarify accountability.

2. *Identify the key variables in the story.*

Problem symptom: **Stress about errors**

Symptomatic solution: **Blame**

Side-effect of symptomatic solution: **Lack of or decrease in sharing information and in communication**

More fundamental solution: **Increase or clarify accountability or communication**

3. *Graph the behavior over time of the symptomatic solution and the fundamental solution.*

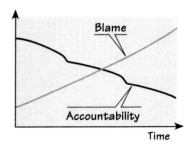

4. *Using the blank systems archetype template, fill in the diagram with the variables you identified. Feel free to add variables to any of the loops. Label each arrow with an "s" or an "o," and add any important delays.*

When errors arise, people often react by wanting to know "who was at fault," because there's a sense that knowing who did it is equivalent to fixing the error itself. So, we go on a "blaming" mission and then feel less stressed about the error when we have located the "culprit." Errors, however, usually are not due to the actions of individuals but more often have to do with their interaction with a system that is not working well. Instead of focusing on the larger issues, blaming guarantees that there will be even less inquiry into and understanding of the system. Hence, the likelihood of errors occurring in the future increases.

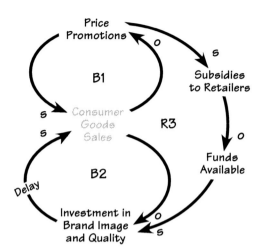

There is usually a delay in the fundamental solution loop—delay in implementing the solution or delay in experiencing the impact of the solution. Your diagram might include one or both types of delay.

ACTIVITY 3   **SHIFTING AUTHORITY THROUGH EMPOWERMENT**

1. *Summarize the "Shifting the Burden" theme in this story in two or three sentences.*

To handle customer complaints, hotel employees have increased authority to take action but do not have authority to focus on overall service quality issues. Their solutions to guest dissatisfaction increase costs, which further detract from investment in service quality. Finally, increased staff authority leads to a growing gap between responsibility and wages, which eventually increases staff resentment, which also reduces service quality.

2. *Identify the key variables in the story.*

Problem that employees can address: **Pressure to respond to guests [to please customers, to maintain customer loyalty]**

Symptomatic solution: **Increased authority for hotel employees**

More fundamental solution: **Improvements in service delivery system**

Unintended side-effects that undermine the fundamental solution: **Increased costs, gap between wages and responsibility, resentment**

3. *Graph the behavior of the symptomatic solution and the fundamental solution.*

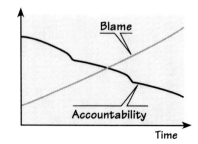

4. *Using the blank systems archetype template, fill in the diagram with the variables you identified. You may want to add additional variables or loops. Label each arrow with an "s" or an "o" and mark any important delays. Label each loop with an "R" or a "B" for "reinforcing" and "balancing."*

Notice that the increased-costs side-effect is shown in one reinforcing loop (R10), and the dynamic of a gap in wages and responsibility leading to increased resentment is shown as an additional loop (R9). This is a slightly more complex version of "Shifting the Burden," but it is not uncommon to have multiple unintended side-effects in this archetype. You can also see how loops B7 and R9 represent a "Fixes That Fail" dynamic.

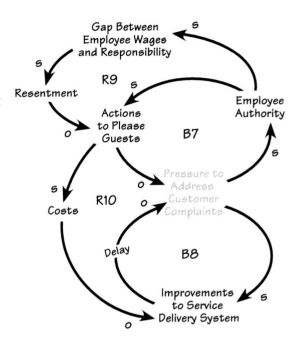

SECTION 4: LIMITS TO SUCCESS

ACTIVITY 1 **LIMITS TO QUALITY**

1. *Summarize the "Limits to Success" theme in this story in two or three sentences.*

The organization worked hard to develop a quality improvement program, and for a while, it was successful. Eventually, though, enthusiasm for quality initiatives lessened, and the program dwindled away. [Your story might mention the constraints of training. However, often when people are first identifying a "Limits to Success" situation, they are less aware of the limiting factors that slowed down or terminated the growth.]

2. *Identify the key variables in the story.*

The growth engine is when **quality improvement projects** begin. As a result, **quality of services** increases, so the **importance of the quality initiative** goes up. **Motivation [to work on quality improvement]** then increases, which reinforces the increase in the original factor.

After a while, the **need for new skills** begins to grow, but it is constrained by **the capacity of the training department**, which reduces the **adequacy of training**. As a result, people do not develop the **ability to implement** the projects, which undermines further growth in improvement projects.

3. *Graph the behavior over time of National Courier's quality initiatives.*

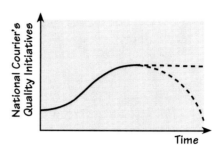

As expected in a "Limits to Success" structure, the number of quality initiatives first grew, slowly and then more rapidly. Eventually, the growth either leveled off or declined. This S-shaped curve is always a clue that "Limits to Success" may be at work, even if the whole story is unclear.

4. *Using the blank systems archetype template, fill in the diagram with the variables. You may add extra variables in any loop. Label all your arrows with an "s" or an "o" to show "same" or "opposite" change.*

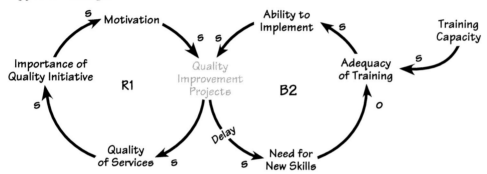

Your causal loop diagram might look different from this one in a couple of ways. You might have more or fewer variables in each of the loops. You might also have more detail related to training capacity, such as training staff and budget. We've combined those variables under "training capacity."

ACTIVITY 2   **CAN RISING SALES HURT IN THE LONG RUN?**

1. *Summarize the "Limits to Success" theme in this story in two or three sentences.*

OCP's strategy is based on the idea that running new marketing campaigns will grow sales, bringing in more revenue and allowing the company to continue and even expand marketing. As a result, the customer base will grow, and OCP will also see growth in toner and service sales. The potential limit to this growth scenario lies in OCP's ability to offer technical assistance in response to new customers' questions about more complex printers. Lack of assistance will drive customers away.

2. *Identify the key variables in the story.*

Engine of growth: **Sales**
                     Revenue
                     Marketing

Limiting process: **Customer base**
                     [Need for technical assistance]
                     Dissatisfaction with this manufacturer

The limiting factor: **Technical assistance capability**

3. *Graph the possible behavior over time of OCP's future sales.*

This graph suggests three possible outcomes for the growth stategy: Sales simply level off; sales gradually decline; or sales decline dramatically. The exact direction of the curve might be influenced by the size of the customer base, the number of people needing assistance, the company's current capacity to provide assistance, the actions of competitors, and the long-term response of customers to poor assistance.

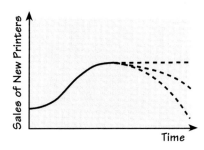

4. *Using the blank systems archetype template, fill in the diagram with the variables you identified. You may have additional variables or loops. Label each of your arrows with an "s" or an "o," and then label each loop in your diagram with an "R" or a "B" to indicate "reinforcing" and "balancing" processes.*

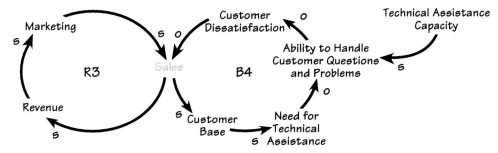

The key to this causal loop diagram is recognizing that "sales" is the variable that links the growth engine and the reinforcing process. Every new sale means more revenue and an increase in the customer base of people who might have questions for technical support staff. We could have left out "need for technical assistance/support" as a separate variable and connected "customer base" directly to "ability to handle customer questions and problems." Choosing one way over the other is always a judgment call about how much detail is necessary to capture the situation accurately and in a way that helps others to understand what is happening.

ACTIVITY 3 ▕ AN INTERNET PROVIDER GETS A BUSY SIGNAL

1. *Summarize the "Limits to Success" theme in this story in two or three sentences.*

SurfBoard set out to grow its customer base, and presumably to increase its market share and revenues, by increasing its marketing and effectively lowering its prices. It succeeded beyond its expectations, with the result that many subscribers could not access SurfBoard's services. Frustrated subscribers created negative press, turned to competitors, and sued SurfBoard, which cost both market share and money.

2. *Identify the key variables in the story.*

Growth mechanism: **Revenues**
Marketing efforts to attract new customers
New customers
Customer base

Limiting process: **Demand for services**
                       Access to services
                       Dissatisfaction / Frustration / Anger
                       [Law suits]
                       [Negative publicity]
                       [Use of competing services]

Limiting factor: **Modem capacity**

3. *Graph the behavior of the variable that SurfBoard wanted to grow.*

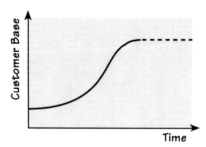

4. *In the space below, draw a causal loop diagram using the variables you identified. Label each arrow with an "s" or an "o," and each loop with an "R" or a "B."*

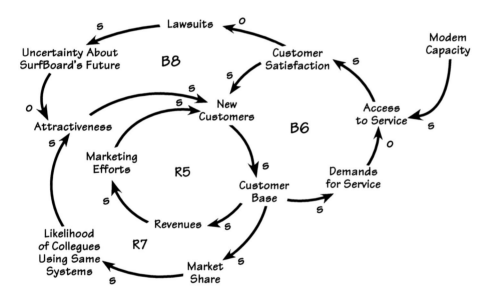

The basic structure shown in this diagram consists of the reinforcing process, Surf-Board's theory about how to grow its business (R5 and R7), and the limiting process stemming from lack of modem capacity, lack of access, and customer dissatisfaction (B6 and B8). Although we could have represented this story with just R5 and B6, the additional loops capture other aspects of the story that are important. They also make the whole picture more compelling and highlight more areas for possible intervention.

SECTION 5: DRIFTING GOALS

ACTIVITY 1 | **THE CASE OF THE DRIFTING PRODUCTION BUDGET**

1. *Summarize the "Drifting Goals" theme in this story in two or three sentences.*

Although there's a goal to keep the project within budget, Maria's desire to impress Corporate and win future work from them keeps pushing her to spend more on each stage of production. Without checking each expenditure along the way, she ends up going over budget.

2. *Identify the key variables in the story.*

The explicit goal was to **keep the project within the budget.**

At several points in the production process, Maria and Franco could have noticed a gap between the goal and **actual expenditures.**

Ideally, they would have **reduced the number of expensive features or options** to stay in line with the goal.

However, they were motivated by pressure to **impress Corporate** and **disregard or change** the original goal.

[As a result, **expenditures** got higher and higher while Corporate was increasingly **delighted or satisfied.**]

3. *Graph what happens over time to the original goal and to the activity it was supposed to control.*

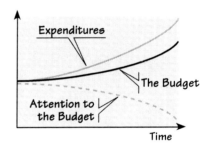

The graph shows two ways of depicting the trend over time in relation to the budget. The upward trending, black line indicates that the budget itself, which was supposed to remain steady, actually increased. The downward trending dashed line shows how attention or adherence to the budget dropped off as the influence of other pressures continued to dominate.

4. *Fill in the blank systems archetype template with the key variables from the story. Label each arrow with an "s" or an "o," and add any important delays.*

The causal loop diagram includes the pressure to impress Corporate as the motivation for the generic pressure to change the goal. The diagram does not depict the consequences that were described in the last sentence in the list of variables. You could show them linked to "number of expensive options," to "actual expenditures," or to "pressure to impress Corporate," depending on your purpose in sharing your mental model.

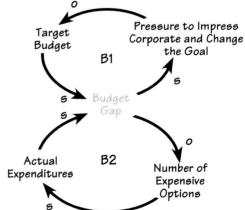

5. *How might Nature Unlimited turn its troubling situation around?*

There are different leverage points, depending on the situation. The first one would be to ask in the project planning meeting what kinds of situations or pressures could cause the project to go off schedule or budget. It might then be possible to manage those variables. Another leverage point would be to educate Corporate about what the production options actually cost, so that their expectations and their payments are aligned. This step would reduce pressure to change the budget.

Other leverage points occur within the production cycle, including more frequent discussions about the status of expenditures and budget. If Maria has difficulty setting expenditure priorities, Franco or Roxanne could get involved in that activity.

SECTION 6: GROWTH AND UNDERINVESTMENT

ACTIVITY 1   THE LOW-COST GROWTH DILEMMA

1. *Summarize the "Growth and Underinvestment" theme in this story in two or three sentences.*

ExpressTech sets out to grow its business by keeping costs down and offering a good product and good service. However, as its business grows, the company is unable to keep up with the need for service—there aren't enough tech support people to handle calls within reasonable time limits. This dilemma probably results from either of two possibilities: a failure to recognize signals to invest in recruiting and training technical staff early enough to have them available as need occurs, or a reluctance to make the necessary level of investment before seeing the revenue.

2. *Identify the key variables in the story.*

[Volume of] sales (the growth variable) was growing, bringing in more and more **revenue**, which financed continued growth. As growth continued, the need for more **technical support or customer service** arose. Based on a **standard of service or standard of response time** (the standard), ExpressTech perceived a growing **need to invest in service personnel or customer service reps**. Although the company responded by increasing **customer service capacity** (the capacity investment variable), there was a **delay** before the effect of the action could be observed.

Notice that delay is included as a variable in this list because of its significant impact on the situation.

3. *Graph what happens over time to the growth variable, the limiting factor, and the capacity investment in the story.*

The sales curve shows the classic S-shape of a "Limits to Success" structure, which is part of a "Growth and Underinvestment" dynamic. This graph shows customer service declining and then improving as sales drop off, easing the pressure on customer service. The investment curve could take many forms, depending on the aggressiveness of the firm's response to the slowdown and subsequent decline in sales.

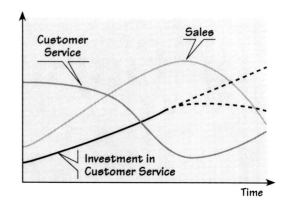

4. *Fill in the blank systems archetype template below with the key variables you identified. Label each arrow with an "s" or an "o," and mark any important delays.*

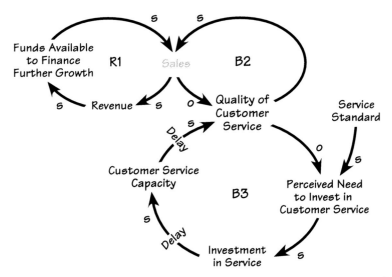

The delay that was identified as a variable is shown in the loop diagram as an intermediate effect between two sets of variables, indicating the extra length of time it will take for the effects of the investment actions to show up. This is how delays are usually depicted in causal loop diagrams.

SECTION 7: SUCCESS TO THE SUCCESSFUL

ACTIVITY 1   **HOOKED ON TECHNOLOGY**

1. *Summarize the "Success to the Successful" theme in this story in two or three sentences.*

   Although the corporate communications department owns two publishing software packages, it favors PubExpress over DeskTop. The more the group uses PubExpress, the less they use DeskTop, to the point of being unwilling to try DeskTop. Even if Desktop is superior to PubExpress, the company will face an uphill battle switching because of the inertia of the "Success to the Successful" dynamic operating for a long time.

2. *Identify the key variables in the story.*

   The resource allocation variable is **use of PubExpress instead of DeskTop.**

   This allocation rationale leads to an increase in **use of PubExpress,** which leads to an increase in **integration of PubExpress into the work process.**

   The allocation rationale also leads to a decrease in **use of DeskTop,** which leads to less **integration of DeskTop into the work process.**

3. *Graph what happens over time to usage of the two software packages.*

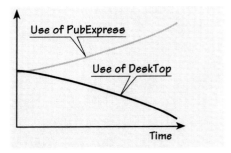

4. Fill in the blank systems archetype template with the variables you identified. Label each arrow with an "s" or an "o."

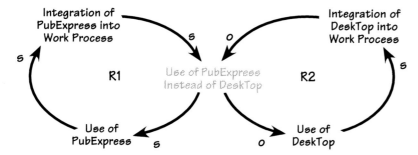

This story illustrates the "competency trap" version of "Success to the Successful." There is nothing inherently wrong with favoring one resource, activity, or investment over another. When a person or organization has adopted one way of doing things, there are definite switching costs associated with changing to a new system. It may not always be worth it to switch to the latest and greatest version to hit the market if the marginal benefits of switching are not worth the costs of making the switch. The question that must be addressed is whether we chose a person, product, or strategy because that will serve the long-run health of the enterprise, or because we are primarily following past practices or history.

SECTION 8: ESCALATION

ACTIVITY 1   ESCALATING BENEFITS

1. *Summarize the "Escalation" theme in this story in two or three sentences.*

   ElCo and DataTech are competing to attract new recruits by offering ever more varied packages of benefits.

2. *Identify the key variables in the story.*

   The central variable is **Elco's attractiveness** over DataTech's.

   The threat is **ability of competing company to attract recruits.**

   The action taken is **improving the benefits for new hires.**

3. *Graph what happens over time to ElCo's and DataTech's success, and to the benefits for new hires.*

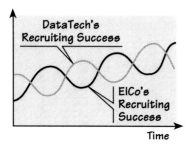

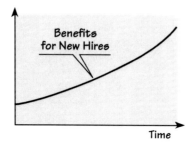

As with all "Escalation" situations, your graph could focus either on the relative positions of the two competitors or on the common factor that escalates. The former creates a picture of how the two are enmeshed in each other's behavior; the latter shows how a variable that may be problematic for both parties is moving out of control.

In the ElCo-DataTech story, the common factor is the benefits package for new hires that rises to a point where the human resources director feels that something needs to be done.

4. *Fill in the blank systems archetype template below with the variables you identified. Label each arrow with an "s" or an "o."*

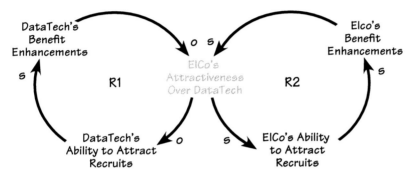

5. *What could DataTech do to de-escalate this situation?*

There are usually at least two possible options for de-escalation: unilaterally withdrawing from the competition by shifting one's emphasis to something that is unique, or enlarging the "pie" to convert a lose/lose situation into a win/win possibility for both parties. DataTech could shift to focusing on its own unique strengths and opportunities as a company so that people will choose to work for them because of the level of alignment they feel with the organization and its people. Alternatively, they could partner with Elco to attract more people into the region as well as keep more people in the region by collaborating to make the region as a whole more attractive.

Section 9: Tragedy of the Commons

Activity 1 **THE TRAGEDY OF THE OVERBURDENED SUPPLIER**

1. *Summarize the "Tragedy of the Commons" theme in this story in two or three sentences.*

One by one, divisions of State Electric & Gas start using workers from TempPower, a regional temporary personnel agency, because they hear that the agency provides high-quality people. Eventually, after several divisions sign up with TempPower, everyone notices a decline in the quality of TempPower workers.

2. *Identify the key variables in the story.*

The Metropolitan division's use of **TempPower workers** goes up, leading to increasing **satisfaction and productivity at Metropolitan,** which prompts them to continue. Then the Southeast division's **use of TempPower workers** begins to rise, and they experience increasing **satisfaction and productivity,** and are encouraged to continue. As both divisions manage their temporary worker needs, their total **use of TempPower workers** increases.

Eventually, this increase encounters **the limit of TempPower's capacity to find and train high-quality temporary workers,** and **the divisions' gain from using TempPower** begins to decline.

3. *Graph what happens over time to the reinforcing process and to the common resource itself.*

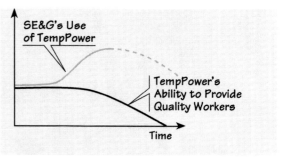

The longer-term outcome of this story is uncertain. TempPower may not be a resource with an absolute limit like the fish population or the electric supply; however, the limit may be considered fixed for the time period of interest. If there is still local labor available, TempPower might simply experience a delay in recruitment and training, but will eventually be able to supply all of SE&G's needs for temporary personnel at the original quality level. On the other hand, if they have depleted all the available supply in the local environs, they will have to invest in pulling people in from far away (not likely for temp work) or they will have to wait for the greater overall job opportunities to increase migration. In this case, their supply is essentially fixed and the dynamics will play out in a more classical "Tragedy of the Commons" pattern.

4. *Fill in the blank systems archetype template below with the variables you identified. Label each arrow in the diagram with an "s" or an "o."*

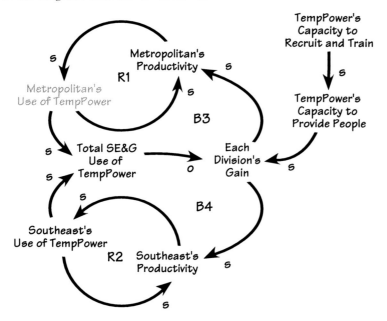

The diagram shows just two of the divisions: Metropolitan and Southeast. The other divisions could be included, stacked above and below Metropolitan and Southeast. You can aggregate and simplify diagrams or elaborate them as necessary to capture your mental model accurately and communicate it effectively. The level of detail and complexity needs to be appropriate for the audience and your purpose in communicating with them. If you want to find out how others see the picture, try starting with a simpler diagram and let them participate in elaborating it. If you want to demonstrate the enormity of the problem, try showing more detail—but be sure not to overwhelm your colleagues.

5. *What can State Electric & Gas do to turn this situation around?*

It would probably be to both divisions' advantage for SE&G to take responsibility for managing the divisions' overall use of TempPower; for example, setting limits on numbers of temporary workers, setting priorities on types of positions filled by temporary workers, or conferring with TempPower about their capacity limits.

SECTION 11: ADDITIONAL LEARNING ACTIVITIES

ACTIVITY 1   REFORMING SCHOOLS

1. *Briefly summarize the point of the story. What theme do you notice? What archetype do you think is at work?*

The excerpt emphasizes the need to focus on fundamental reform in education. Otherwise, we may reform the wrong things and do more harm than good. The emphasis on fundamental reform suggests the "Shifting the Burden" archetype.

2. *Identify the key variables in the example at the end of the story.*

Test scores [performance on exams]
Focus on exam-taking techniques
Belief in performing, not learning
Efforts to engage students' interest in learning

3. *Graph the behavior over time of those variables.*

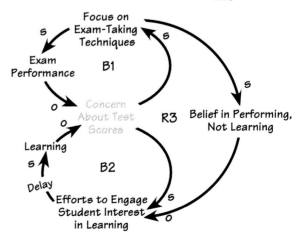

4. *Using the variables, create a causal loop diagram. If you discover an additional variable, include it in your diagram and add it to the list of variables. When you complete the diagram, walk through it with the story to make sure it depicts the dynamics. Also check the diagram against your BOT graph to ensure that it captures the changes that occur over time.*

5. *Looking at the diagram, what archetype do you see?*

This is a classic "Shifting the Burden" archetypal structure, with its "quick fix" and fundamental solution, and the unintended side-effect that detracts from the fundamental solution.

6. *What other archetypes might be involved in this situation?*

This story could also be seen as a "Fixes That Fail," in which the "quick fix" is the focus on exam-taking techniques, leading to an improvement in exam performance. Then the unintended side-effect might be something like "emphasis on irrelevant standards," which eventually causes exam performance to fall again.

7. *Are there any archetypes that might come into play in the future?*

Another archetype that might be at work in this situation is "Drifting Goals." Educational standards or even standards for performance on exams could come under pressure to be lowered. In a sense, this story also has the flavor of "Success to the Successful." An emphasis on exam performance instead of learning has caused more attention to go toward exam-taking skills (along with rewarding those who are good exam takers with academic and job success) and less toward genuine improvements in learning.

8. *What are the management or intervention guidelines suggested by the archetypes you identified?*

The "Shifting the Burden" archetype reminds us to manage both halves of the dynamic—we need to continue to pay some attention to standardized exams while we also implement improved strategies for real learning. This archetype also encourages us to really understand why the public is drawn to the various quick fixes and is not willing to acknowledge or support the longer-term, fundamental fixes. Perhaps sharper awareness of the problems in education is needed; perhaps a public information campaign would help.

"Drifting Goals" reminds us to refocus and recommit to the goals, which is also helpful in redirecting a "Shifting the Burden" dynamic.

"Success to the Successful" encourages us to look at the bigger picture, at the overarching goal that might unite both halves of the dynamic.

ACTIVITY 2   **CUSTOMER SERVICE DILEMMAS**

1. *Briefly summarize the theme(s) you notice in the story. What archetype or archetypes do you think is or are at work?*

Sales increase, which increases pressures. At first, people work harder, but eventually the pressure is too much, and quality suffers. When quality dips, advertisers withdraw, and pressure goes down.

The story sounds like "Drifting Goals"—when the time pressure gets bad, the normal quality standard is reduced, or dumped completely.

2. *Identify the key variables from the story. You may find that two or more variables can be aggregated into a single higher-level variable.*

Sales
Advertisers' demand [calls, requests]
[Time] Pressure
Improvement efforts
Productivity
Morale
Errors
Work completed
Quality
Advertiser satisfaction

3. *Graph the behavior over time of those variables.*

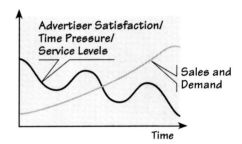

4. *Using the variables, create a causal loop diagram. If you discover an additional variable, include it in your diagram and add it to the list of variables. When you complete the diagram, walk through it with the story to make sure it depicts the dynamics. Also check it against your BOT graph to ensure that it captures the changes that occur over time.*

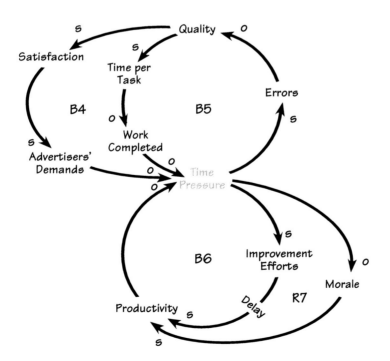

In this diagram, notice the reinforcing process (R7) that includes the impact of dropping morale. Also notice that the problem can appear to "solve itself" by engaging loop B4 where customer dissatisfaction leads to lower demand, hence lower time pressure.

5. *Looking at the diagram, what archetypes do you notice?*

In addition to a dynamic like "Drifting Goals," this structure has a "Fixes That Fail" component. Increasing effort to be more productive in response to time pressures works only for a while. After a certain point, time pressure causes morale to decline, which means that less work gets done and time pressure gets worse. At that point, the "Drifting Goals" phenomenon kicks in, and quality standards drop. Satisfaction and demand go down, and the pressure is relieved.

6. *Are there any other archetypes that might come into play in the future?*

Over the long haul, this structure could begin to work like the "death spiral" in "Limits to Success." The reinforcing loop that includes morale could cause quality and satisfaction levels to erode faster than sales could bring advertisers back to the paper.

7. *What are the management or intervention guidelines suggested by the archetypes you identified?*

"Drifting Goals" focuses us on holding to the standards and creating the structures in our organization that allow us to meet the standard. The newspaper may need to reengineer some of its processes and find ways to bring in part-time or temporary workers.

The "Fixes That Fail" structure points out the need to look at the longer-term consequences of a proposed solution. In this story, the "proposed solution" is simply the natural response of the service group to increased pressure. Management needs to consider alternative approaches to responding to increasing pressure.

Finally, the reinforcing nature of the periodic morale/productivity/quality drops indicates that the problem could jeopardize the newspaper's future advertising revenue. It also suggests that it is important enough to merit serious attention.

ACTIVITY 3   BALANCING WORK AND FAMILY

1. *Briefly summarize the theme(s) in the story. What archetype(s) do you think might be at work?*

The more time you put into your work project, the better things get at work and the worse things get at home. The story sounds like a "Success to the Successful" situation where one activity has a tendency to dominate the other.

2. *Identify the key variables in the story. You may find that two or more variables may be aggregated into a single higher-level variable.*

Priority of work over home/family [Desire to be at work instead of home]
Time at work
Success at work
Time at home [Time with family]
Tension at home [with family]
Success at home

3. *Graph the behavior over time of those variables.*

Notice that you can aggregate all the work-related variables under the central variable:"Priority of work over home/family." You can also aggregate the family-related variables to show the opposite, downward trend.

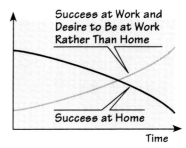

4. *Using the variables, create a causal loop diagram. If you discover an additional variable, include it in your diagram and add it to the list of variables. When you complete the diagram, walk through it with the story to make sure it depicts the dynamics. Also check it against your BOT graph to ensure that it captures the changes that occur over time.*

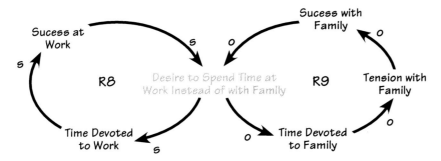

5. *Looking at the diagram, what archetypes do you notice?*

This is a classic "Success to the Successful" structure, in which increasing satisfaction with work leads to more and more time and attention devoted to it, and decreasing satisfaction with home life leads to less and less time and attention spent there.

6. *Are there any other archetypes that might come into play in the future?*

Whenever there is increasing growth in a reinforcing process, "Limits to Success" comes to mind. What will be the limit to the growing satisfaction at work? Is there a limit to the amount of time that can be spent? the level of success? Or will the limit result from the family's total disintegration?

7. *What are the management or intervention guidelines suggested by the archetypes you identified?*

"Success to the Successful" reminds us to return to the bigger picture and the overarching goal. If the higher goal is to have a balanced life, we are reminded to change priorities or somehow put boundaries around the hours devoted to work.

"Limits to Success" is a reminder to consider that whatever growing, expanding, improving trend we're experiencing in the present is unlikely to last forever. In the case of balancing work and family life, we need to understand that the trend toward devoting more and more time to work has a limit.

ACTIVITY 4   **GETTING WHAT YOU MEASURE**

1. *Briefly summarize the theme(s) in the story. What archetype(s) do you think might be at work?*

    It seems as if the better managers get at finding and solving local problems, the more successful they are and the more local problems there are to be solved. On the other hand, in-depth analysis is not encouraged at all.

    "Shifting the Burden" seems to be involved.

2. *Identify the key variables in the story. You may find that two or more variables may be aggregated into a single higher-level variable.*

    Recalls of central staff
    "SWAT team" visits
    Likelihood of getting requested budget
    Use of senior executives' preferred indicators
    Problem symptoms
    Quick fixes
    In-depth analysis
    Proactive measures

3. *Graph the behavior over time of those variables.*

    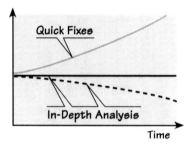

    Notice that this graph could be very busy, with each variable that shows a rising tendency graphed separately. The trend for in-depth analysis and proactive measures is harder to draw—is it flat? declining? The key is that it is not growing.

4. *Using the variables, create a causal loop diagram. If you discover an additional variable, include it in your diagram and add it to the list of variables. When you complete the diagram, walk through it with the story to make sure it depicts the dynamics. Also check it against your BOT graph to ensure that it captures the changes that occur over time.*

    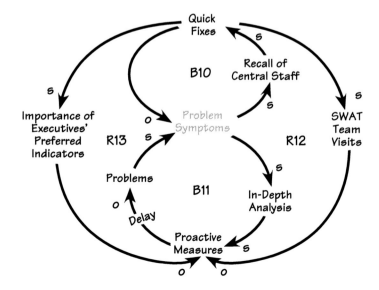

5. *Looking at the diagram, what archetypes do you notice?*

The "Shifting the Burden" dynamic shows up in the organization's preference for quick fixes and "SWAT team" missions rather than in-depth analysis, planning, and proactive strategies. The delay involved in implementing the more fundamental approaches is likely to make it difficult to reverse these practices.

6. *Are there any other archetypes that might come into play in the future?*

Additional negative unintended consequences may develop, such as increasing inability to even perform in-depth analysis and take proactive measures.

A form of "Success to the Successful" may already be at work in the way budget allocation is done. Managers who find and solve problems immediately are rewarded; this dynamic implies that managers who are inclined to take longer-term approaches are not as well rewarded.

7. *What are the management or intervention guidelines suggested by the archetypes you identified?*

Once again, "Shifting the Burden" implies a need to balance short-term interventions with more fundamental changes rather than a sudden switch from one focus to the other. In this situation, the senior executives may need to refocus their vision and identify the appropriate indicators that will serve their vision.

ACTIVITY 5 · SURVIVING COMPETITION

1. *Briefly summarize the theme(s) in the story. What archetype(s) do you think might be at work?*

Parker Roberts was growing and then ran into problems. The company is proposing a variety of strategies for recapturing their growth. Sounds like both "Limits to Success" and "Fixes That Fail."

2. *Identify the key variables in the story.*

   Price-to-performance ratio
   Sales [revenue]
   Product development & engineering breakthroughs
   Financial pressure
   Use of outside supplier [parts]
   Costs
   Margin
   Net income
   Premium [brand] image
   Price
   Use of multiple distribution channels

3. *Graph the behavior over time of those variables.*

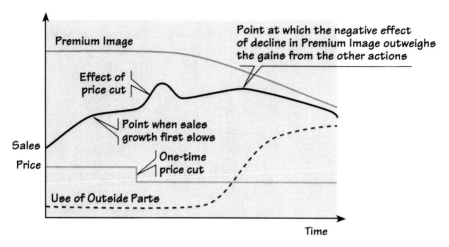

Note that in a complex problem like this one, you may select only certain variables to graph—perhaps the ones that represent the core of the story, perhaps the ones that represent the outcomes of various proposed strategies, or perhaps variables that represent the aggregate dynamics of two or three other variables.

4. *Using the variables, create a causal loop diagram. If you discover an additional variable, include it in your diagram and add it to the list of variables. (Note: This is a complex story. You might find it easiest to diagram "episodes" of the story, one at a time, and then link them up.) When you complete the diagram, walk through it with the story to make sure it depicts the dynamics. Also check it against your BOT graph to ensure that it captures the changes that occur over time.*

This diagram consists of eight loops: four reinforcing ones, and four balancing processes.

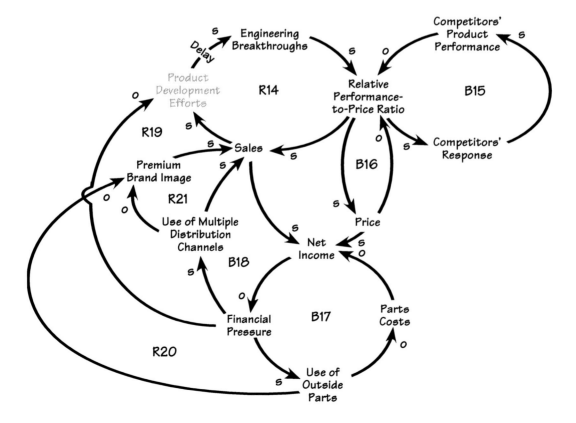

5. *Looking at the diagram, what archetypes do you notice?*

If we consider the diagram as a whole, it represents a very complex "Limits to Success" structure, where R14 is the primary growth engine and the other loops are all producing slowing actions. When we look at the details of the loops, we can also identify three "Fixes That Fail" structures: B16 and R19; B17 and R20; and B18 and R21. As as "Limits to Success" structure, the reinforcing loop of product development efforts—>engineering breakthroughs—>relative performance to price ratio—>sales drives the initial growth (R14). A relatively high ratio drives competitors to respond by increasing their performance so that they can attract more customers (B15).

One of the quickest ways to increase the ratio is to lower the price (B16). This action improves the performance-to-price picture immediately. There are, however, other consequences that can be triggered that will produce undesirable long-term results. The price cuts can reduce net income if unit volume does not increase enough to cover the price reductions. Even if sales rise in the short run, lower prices means lower margins, which will increase the financial pressure. Because of tighter margins, we may cut back on the percentage we spend on product development, which will end up reinforcing the need to cut prices to stay ahead of the competition (R19). This is the first of the three "Fixes That Fail."

The second "Fixes That Fail" is launched when we respond to financial pressure by increasing the use of outside parts. It does have the immediate effect of reducing parts costs and improving our net income figure (B17). The longer-term failure may come in the deterioration of the premium brand image, which will end up reducing sales (R20). The third "Fixes That Fail" happens when we expand distribution channels, which may initially improve sales (B18). However, if this move reduces our premium image, sales will suffer in the long run (R21).

6. *Are there any other archetypes that might come into play in the future?*

The balancing loop containing the "financial pressure" variable is a reminder that it is easy to fall into "Shifting the Burden" when we experience uncomfortable pressures. It could be helpful to consider whether there are more fundamental solutions to address the costs and margin issues.

A fall in revenues after a growth spurt is a reminder to check for aspects of "Growth and Underinvestment." Is there some fundamental capacity that Parker Roberts needs to invest in to support future growth?

Lowering prices suggests the value of checking for a "Drifting Goals" phenomenon to help the company avoid sliding from a premium brand to just another commodity producer.

7. *What are the management or intervention guidelines suggested by the archetypes you identified?*

"Fixes That Fail" points out the need to look at the bigger picture and the longer term before adopting a response to competitive pressure. "Limits to Success" is a reminder to continue looking for the limiting capabilities that could arise to slow down or reverse growth.

A Palette of Systems Thinking Tools

BRAINSTORMING TOOLS

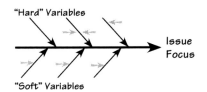

DOUBLE-Q DIAGRAM

Captures free-flowing thoughts in a structured manner, and distinguishes between "hard" and "soft" variables that affect the issue of interest.

DYNAMIC THINKING TOOLS

BEHAVIOR OVER TIME GRAPH

Can be used to graph the behavior of each variable over time and gain insights into any interrelationships between them. (BOT diagrams are also known as reference mode diagrams.)

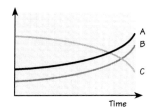

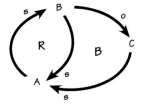

CAUSAL LOOP DIAGRAM

Captures how variables in a system are interrelated, using cause-and-effect linkages. Can help you identify reinforcing (R) and balancing (B) processes.

SYSTEMS ARCHETYPE

Helps you recognize common system behavior patterns such as "Drifting Goals," "Shifting the Burden," "Limits to Success," "Fixes That Fail," and so on—all the compelling, recurring "stories" of organizational dynamics.

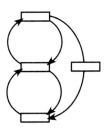

STRUCTURAL THINKING TOOLS

GRAPHICAL FUNCTION DIAGRAM

Captures the way in which one variable affects another, by plotting the relationship between the two over the full range of relevant values.

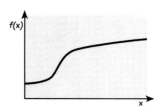

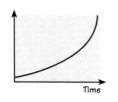

STRUCTURE-BEHAVIOR PAIR

Consists of the basic dynamic structures that can serve as building blocks for developing computer models (for example, exponential growth, delays, smooths, S-shaped growth, oscillations, and so on).

POLICY STRUCTURE DIAGRAM

A conceptual map of the decision-making process embedded in the organization. Focuses on the factors that are weighed for each decision, and can be used to build a library of generic structures.

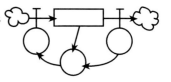

COMPUTER-BASED TOOLS

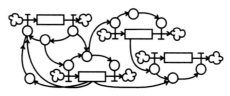

COMPUTER MODEL

Lets you translate all relationships identified as relevant into mathematical equations. You can then run policy analyses through multiple simulations.

MANAGEMENT FLIGHT SIMULATOR

Provides "flight training" for managers through the use of interactive computer games based on a computer model. Users can recognize long-term consequences of decisions by formulating strategies and making decisions based on those strategies.

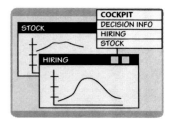

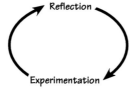

LEARNING LABORATORY

A manager's practice field. Is equivalent to a sports team's experience, which blends active experimentation with reflection and discussion. Uses all the systems thinking tools, from double-Q diagrams to MFSs.

APPENDIX C

Systems Archetypes at a Glance

Fixes That Fail

In a "Fixes That Fail" situation, a problem symptom cries out for resolution. A solution is quickly implemented, which alleviates the symptom. However, the solution produces unintended consequences that, after a delay, cause the original problem symptom to return to its previous level or even get worse. This development leads us to apply the same (or similar) fix again. This reinforcing cycle of fixes is the essence of "Fixes That Fail."

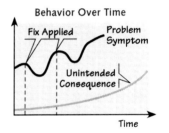

Guidelines

- Breaking a "Fixes That Fail" cycle usually requires acknowledging that the fix is merely alleviating a symptom, and making a commitment to solve the real problem now.

- A two-pronged attack of applying the fix and planning out the fundamental solution will help ensure that you don't get caught in a perpetual cycle of solving yesterday's "solutions."

Shifting the Burden

In a "Shifting the Burden" situation, a problem symptom can be addressed by applying a symptomatic solution or a more fundamental solution. When a symptomatic solution is implemented, the problem symptom is reduced or disappears, which lessens the pressure for implementing a more fundamental solution. Over time, the symptom resurfaces, and another round of symptomatic solutions is implemented in a vicious, figure-8 reinforcing cycle. The symptomatic solutions often produce side-effects that further divert attention away from more fundamental solutions.

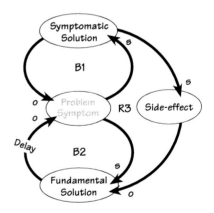

Guidelines

- Problem symptoms are usually easier to recognize than the other elements of the structure.

- If the side-effect has become the problem, you may be dealing with an "Addiction" structure.

- Whether a solution is "symptomatic" or "fundamental" often depends on one's perspective. Explore the problem from differing perspectives in order to come to a more comprehensive understanding of what the fundamental solution may be.

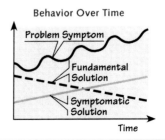

Limits to Success

In a "Limits to Success" scenario, growing actions initially lead to success, which encourages even more of those efforts. Over time, however, the success itself causes the system to encounter limits, which slows down improvements in results. As the success triggers the limiting action and performance declines, the tendency is to focus even more on the initial growing actions.

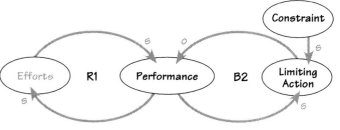

Guidelines

- The archetype is most helpful when it is used well in advance of any problems, to see how the cumulative effects of continued success might lead to future problems.

- Use the archetype to explore questions such as, "What kinds of pressures are building up in the organization as a result of the growth?"

- Look for ways to relieve pressures or remove limits before an organizational gasket blows.

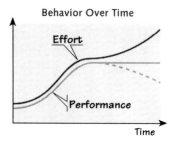

Drifting Goals

In a "Drifting Goals" situation, a gap between desired performance and current reality can be resolved either by taking corrective action to achieve the goal or by lowering the goal. The gap is often resolved by a gradual lowering of the goal. Over time, the performance level also drifts downward. This drift may happen so gradually, even without deliberate action, that the organization is not even aware of its impact.

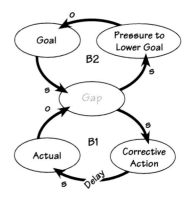

Guidelines

- Drifting performance figures are usually indicators that the "Drifting Goals" archetype is at work and that real corrective actions are not being taken.

- A critical aspect of avoiding a potential "Drifting Goals" scenario is to determine what drives the setting of the goals.

- Goals located outside the system will be less susceptible to drifting goals pressures.

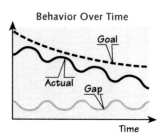

Growth and Underinvestment

In a "Growth and Underinvestment" situation, growth approaches a limit that could be eliminated or postponed if capacity investments were made. Instead, as a result of policies or delays in the system, demand (or performance) degrades, limiting further growth. The declining demand then leads to further withholding of investment or even reductions in capacity, causing even worse performance.

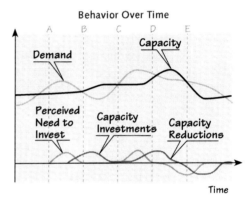

Guidelines

• Dig into the assumptions that drive capacity investment decisions. If past performance dominates as a consideration, try to balance that perspective with a fresh look at demand and the factors that drive its growth.

• If there is a potential for growth, build capacity in anticipation of future demand.

Success to the Successful

In a "Success to the Successful" situation, two or more individuals, groups, projects, initiatives, etc. are vying for a limited pool of resources to achieve success. If one of them starts to become more successful (or is historically already more successful) than the others, it tends to garner more resources, thereby increasing the likelihood of continued success. Its initial success justifies devoting more resources while robbing the other alternatives of resources and opportunities to build their own success, even if the others are superior alternatives.

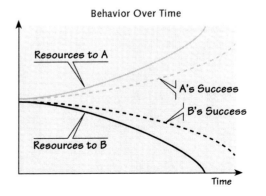

Guidelines

• Look for reasons why the system was set up to create just one "winner."

• Chop off one half of the archetype by focusing efforts and resources on one group, rather than creating a "winner-take-all" competition.

• Find ways to make teams collaborators rather than competitors.

• Identify goals or objectives that define success at a level higher than the individual players A and B.

Escalation

In an "Escalation" situation, one party (A) takes actions to counter a perceived threat. These actions are then perceived by the other party (B) as creating an imbalance in the system that then makes them feel threatened. So, B responds to close the gap, creating an imbalance from A's perspective, and on it goes. The dynamic of two parties, each trying to achieve a sense of "safety," becomes an overall reinforcing process that escalates tension on both sides, tracing a figure-8 pattern with the two balancing loops in this archetype.

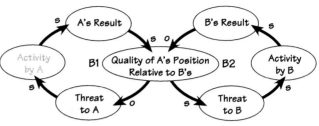

Guidelines To break an escalation structure, ask the following questions:

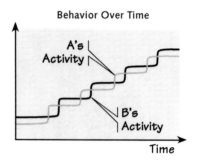

Behavior Over Time

- What is the relative measure that pits one party against the other, and can you change it?

- What are the significant delays in the system that may distort the true nature of the threat?

- What are the deep-rooted assumptions that lie beneath the actions taken in response to the threat?

Tragedy of the Commons

In a "Tragedy of the Commons" situation, individuals make use of a common resource by pursuing actions for their own enjoyment or benefit, without concern for the collective impact of everyone's actions. At some point, the sum of all individual activity overloads the "commons," and all parties involved experience diminishing benefits. The commons may even collapse.

Guidelines

- Effective solutions for a "Tragedy of the Commons" scenario never lie at the individual level.

- Ask questions such as: "What are the incentives for individuals to persist in their actions?" "Can the long-term collective loss be made more real and immediate to the individual actors?"

- Find ways to reconcile short-term individual rewards with long-term cumulative consequences. A governing body that is chartered with the sustainability of the resource limit can help.

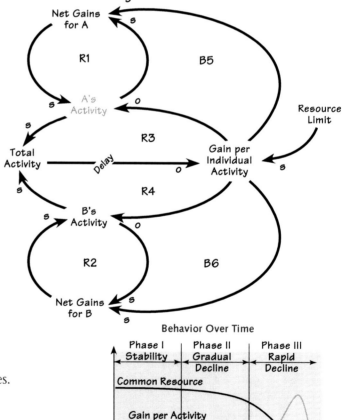

Behavior Over Time

Additional Resources

Newsletters

The Systems Thinker® (Pegasus Communications)

Leverage Points for a New Workplace, New World® (Pegasus Communications)

Books

The Fifth Discipline: The Art and Practice of the Learning Organization, Peter M. Senge (Doubleday, 1990)

The Fifth Discipline Fieldbook, Peter Senge et al. (Doubleday, 1994)

The Systems Thinking Playbook, Linda Booth Sweeney and Dennis Meadows (The Turning Point Foundation, 1996)

Billibonk and the Big Itch, Philip Ramsey (Pegasus Communications, 1998)

Short Volumes

Systems Archetypes I: Diagnosing Systemic Issues and Designing High-Leverage Interventions, Daniel H. Kim (Pegasus Communications, 1992)

Systems Archetypes II: Using Systems Archetypes to Take Effective Action, Daniel H. Kim (Pegasus Communications, 1994)

Systems Thinking Tools: A User's Reference Guide, Daniel H. Kim (Pegasus Communications, 1994)

Applying Systems Archetypes, Daniel H. Kim and Colleen Lannon (Pegasus Communications, 1996)

Designing a Systems Thinking Intervention: A Strategy for Leveraging Change, Michael Goodman et al. (Pegasus Communications, 1997)

The Tale of Windfall Abbey, Margaret Welbank (BP Exploration Operating Company Limited, 1992)

Laminated Reference Guides

Systems Archetypes at a Glance (Pegasus Communications)

A Pocket Guide to Using the Archetypes (Pegasus Communications)

Archetype Display Set (Pegasus Communications)

A Glossary of Systems Thinking Terms

Systems thinking can serve as a language for communicating about complexity and interdependencies. To be fully conversant in any language, you must gain some mastery of the vocabulary, especially the phrases and idioms unique to that language. This glossary lists many terms that may come in handy when you're faced with a systems problem.

Accumulator Anything that builds up or dwindles; for example, water in a bathtub, savings in a bank account, inventory in a warehouse. In modeling software, a stock is often used as a generic symbol for accumulators. Also known as **Stock** or **Level.**

Balancing Process/Loop Combined with reinforcing loops, balancing processes form the building blocks of dynamic systems. Balancing processes seek equilibrium: They try to bring things to a desired state and keep them there. They also limit and constrain change generated by reinforcing processes. A balancing loop in a causal loop diagram depicts a balancing process.

Balancing Process with Delay A commonly occurring structure. When a balancing process has a long delay, the usual response is to *over*correct. Over-correction leads to wild swings in behavior. Example: real estate cycles.

Behavior Over Time (BOT) Graph One of the 10 tools of systems thinking. BOT graphs capture the history or trend of one or more variables over time. By sketching several variables on one graph, you can gain an explicit understanding of how they interact over time. Also called **Reference Mode.**

Causal Loop Diagram (CLD) One of the 10 tools of systems thinking. Causal loop diagrams capture how variables in a system are interrelated. A CLD takes the form of a closed loop that depicts cause-and-effect linkages.

Drifting Goals A systems archetype. In a "Drifting Goals" scenario, a gradual downward slide in performance goals goes unnoticed, threatening the long-term future of the system or organization. Example: lengthening delivery delays.

Escalation A systems archetype. In the "Escalation" archetype, two parties compete for superiority in an arena. As one party's actions put it ahead, the other party "retaliates" by increasing its actions. The result is a continual ratcheting up of activity on both sides. Examples: price battles, the Cold War.

Feedback The return of information about the status of a process. Example: annual performance reviews return information to an employee about the quality of his or her work.

Fixes That Fail A systems archetype. In a "Fixes That Fail" situation, a fix is applied to a problem and has immediate positive results. However, the fix also has unforeseen long-term consequences that eventually worsen the problem. Also known as "Fixes That Backfire."

Flow The amount of change something undergoes during a particular unit of time. Example: the amount of water that flows out of a bathtub each minute, or the amount of interest earned in a savings account each month. Also called a **Rate**.

Generic Structures Structures that can be generalized across many different settings because the underlying relationships are fundamentally the same. Systems archetypes are a class of generic structures.

Graphical Function Diagram (GFD) One of the 10 tools of systems thinking. GFDs show how one variable, such as delivery delays, interacts with another, such as sales, by plotting the relationship between the two over the entire range of relevant values. The resulting diagram is a concise hypothesis of how the two variables interrelate. Also called **Table Function**.

Growth and Underinvestment A systems archetype. In this situation, resource investments in a growing area are not made, owing to short-term pressures. As growth begins to stall because of lack of resources, there is less incentive for adding capacity, and growth slows even further.

Learning Laboratory One of the 10 tools of systems thinking. A learning laboratory embeds a management flight simulator in a learning environment. Groups of managers use a combination of systems thinking tools to explore the dynamics of a particular system and inquire into their own understanding of that system. Learning labs serve as a manager's practice field.

Level See **Accumulator**.

Leverage Point An area where small change can yield large improvements in a system.

Limits to Success A systems archetype. In a "Limits to Success" scenario, a company or product line grows rapidly at first, but eventually begins to slow or even decline. The reason is that the system has hit some limit—capacity constraints, resource limits, market saturation, etc.—that is inhibiting further growth. Also called "Limits to Growth."

Management Flight Simulator (MFS) One of the 10 tools of systems thinking. Similar to a pilot's flight simulator, an MFS allows managers to test the outcome of different policies and decisions without "crashing and burning" real companies. An MFS is based on a system dynamics computer model that has been changed into an interactive decision-making simulator through the use of a user interface.

Policy Structure Diagram One of the 10 tools of systems thinking. Policy structure diagrams are used to create a conceptual "map" of the decision-making process that is embedded in an organization. It highlights the factors that are weighed at each decision point.

Rate See **Flow**.

Reference Mode See **Behavior Over Time Graph.**

Reinforcing Process/Loop Along with balancing loops, reinforcing loops form the building blocks of dynamic systems. Reinforcing processes compound change in one direction with even more change in that same direction. As such, they generate both growth and collapse. A reinforcing loop in a causal loop diagram depicts a reinforcing process. Also known as vicious cycles or virtuous cycles.

Shifting the Burden A systems archetype. In a "Shifting the Burden" situation, a short-term solution is tried that successfully solves an ongoing problem. As the solution is used over and over again, it takes attention away from more fundamental, enduring solutions. Over time, the ability to apply a fundamental solution may decrease, resulting in more and more reliance on the symptomatic solution. Examples: drug and alcohol dependency.

Shifting the Burden to the Intervener A special case of the "Shifting the Burden" systems archetype that occurs when an intervener is brought in to help solve an ongoing problem. Over time, as the intervener successfully handles the problem, the people within the system become less capable of solving the problem themselves. They become even more dependent on the intervener. Example: ongoing use of outside consultants.

Simulation Model One of the 10 tools of systems thinking. A computer model that lets you map the relationships that are important to a problem or an issue and then simulate the interaction of those variables over time.

Stock See **Accumulator.**

Structural Diagram Draws out the accumulators and flows in a system, giving an overview of the major structural elements that produce the system's behavior. Also called flow diagram or accumulator/flow diagram.

Structure-Behavior Pair One of the 10 tools of systems thinking. A structure-behavior pair consists of a structural representation of a business issue, using accumulators and flows, and the corresponding behavior over time (BOT) graph for the issue being studied.

Structure The manner in which a system's elements are organized or interrelated. The structure of an organization, for example, could include not only the organizational chart but also incentive systems, information flows, and interpersonal interactions.

Success to the Successful A systems archetype. In a "Success to the Successful" situation, two activities compete for a common but limited resource. The activity that is *initially* more successful is consistently given more resources, allowing it to succeed even more. At the same time, the activity that is *initially* less successful becomes starved for resources and eventually dies out. Example: the QWERTY layout of typewriter keyboards.

System Dynamics A field of study that includes a methodology for constructing computer simulation models to achieve better understanding of social and corporate systems. It draws on organizational studies, behavioral decision theory, and engineering to provide a theoretical and empirical base for structuring the relationships in complex systems.

System A group of interacting, interrelated, or interdependent elements forming a complex whole. Almost always defined with respect to a specific purpose within a larger system. Example: An R&D department is a system that has a purpose in the context of the larger organization.

Systems Archetypes One of the 10 tools of systems thinking. Systems archetypes are the "classic stories" in systems thinking—common patterns and structures that occur repeatedly in different settings.

Systems Thinking A school of thought that focuses on recognizing the interconnections between the parts of a system and synthesizing them into a unified view of the whole.

Table Function See **Graphical Function Diagram.**

Template A tool used to identify systems archetypes. To use a template, you fill in the blank variables in causal loop diagrams.

Tragedy of the Commons A systems archetype. In a "Tragedy of the Commons" scenario, a shared resource becomes overburdened as each person in the system uses more and more of the resource for individual gain. Eventually, the resource dwindles or is wiped out, resulting in lower gains for everyone involved. Example: the Greenhouse Effect.

The above glossary is a compilation of definitions from many sources, including:
- Innovation Associates' and GKA's Introduction to Systems Thinking coursebooks
- *The Fifth Discipline: The Art and Practice of the Learning Organization,* by Peter Senge
- High Performance Systems' *Academic User's Guide to STELLA*
- *The American Heritage Dictionary* and *The Random House Dictionary.*